The Rhetoric of the "Other" Literature

W. Ross Winterowd

Southern Illinois University Press
Carbondale and Edwardsville

Edited by Mara Lou Hawse
Designed by Shannon M. McIntyre
Production supervised by Natalia Nadraga

Library of Congress Cataloging-in-Publication Data

Winterowd, W. Ross.
  The rhetoric of the "other" literature / W. Ross Winterowd.
    p.   cm.
  Bibliography: p.
  Includes index.
  ISBN 0-8093-1587-4
  1. Reportage literature, American—History and criticism.
2. American prose literature—20th century—History and criticism—
Theory, etc. 3. Journalism—United States—History—20th century.
4. Rhetoric—History—20th century. 5. Canon (Literature)
6. Nonfiction novel. 7. Literary form. I. Title.
PS366.R44W56   1990

818'.50809—dc20   89-33261
                                                                   CIP

Chapter 5, "Form: The Essay," is adapted from "Rediscovering the Essay,"
Journal of Advanced Composition 8 (1988): 146–57. Reprinted by permission.

Late Night Thoughts While Listening to Mahler's Ninth Symphony by Lewis
Thomas. Copyright © 1982 by Lewis Thomas. All rights reserved.
Reprinted by permission of Viking Penguin, a division of Penguin Books
USA, Inc.

The paper used in this publication meets the minimum requirements of
American National Standard for Information Sciences —Permanence
of Paper for Printed Library Materials, ANSI Z39.48-1984. ⊚

For *John and Tilly Warnock*

Contents

Introduction:
The Phantasmagoria of the Text

These pages are moments in the ceaseless flow of textuality. They discuss what is now called "the nonfiction novel" (e.g., *In Cold Blood*) and "the New Journalism"; essays, a variety of which I term "lyrics in prose" (e.g., Loren Eiseley's "The Angry Winter"); "the confession," again my term (e.g., *Armies of the Night*); and "the nature meditation" (e.g., *The Snow Leopard, Pilgrim at Tinker Creek*).

The greatest problem, perhaps, is finding a term that covers the texts I deal with in this book. "The literature of fact"? But factuality is not really a central issue. "Non-imaginative literature"? Hardly, since one of my purposes is to argue that the texts I discuss are just as imaginative as the poems, stories, novels, and plays that are generally considered to constitute "imaginative" literature.

Actually, throughout my planning and writing of this book, I have been preoccupied with the question of terminology, and finally, now that I am saying my last say, I have decided merely to surrender. I am dealing with the "other" literature, and I will title the book *The Rhetoric of the "Other" Literature*. I will use terms such as "the literature of fact" and "non-imaginative literature" simply because I can find no others.

Was it not inevitable that a book studying the rhetoric of nonfiction would appear at this time in history? Nonfiction literature—or "the literature" of fact—is being rehabilitated within the literary establishment, and rhetoric is being repatriated after nearly a century of exile from the literary establishment. J. Hillis Miller speaks of "the sort of rhetorical analysis of works of literature I and some others try to do" (*Ethics* 9). Kenneth Burke is at last gaining the respect he deserves. Much of the most interesting work in linguistics—such as Kochman's *Black and White Styles in Conflict*—might as well be called rhetorical study.

Certainly my book on the rhetoric of nonfiction genres will provide the occasion for a response or elaboration, a study of the rhetoric of fiction which might, indeed, be called just that: *The Rhetoric of Fiction*. This book would presumably study the ways whereby authors influence readers of fiction. It would debunk anti-rhetorical dogma, such as the dictum that authors should show, not tell; it would also deal with the problems of narration, undoubtedly attempting to clarify stances such as that of the unreliable narrator; most important, perhaps, it would be a counterstatement to much of the literary theory that has held literary works to be autonomous and would (since its standpoint would be rhetorical) even discuss morality in fiction.

In one sense, this book is extremely traditional, its purpose being to apply the principles of rhetoric to literary explication and to reestablish an important part of the canon.

The question is definitely not "What is this text?" Rather, one asks, "What can I take this text to be?" That is, "What sort of illocutionary force do I attribute to this text?"

The attribution cannot be perfectly free and yet be perfectly felicitous. If, for instance, I claim (in the context of this introduction) that the following is a lyric poem, readers will necessarily either ignore my statement or somehow rationalize it (e.g., take it as metaphor or irony):

> Each file on a diskette must have a different name. DOS uses the file name to find the file on the diskette.
> In DOS, file names contain 1 to 8 characters. The characters in a file name can be any of the following:
> * Letters of the alphabet A through Z
> * Numerals 0 through 9
> * Special characters:
> $#&@!%(){}'—-
>
> —*IBM PC Convertible Guide to Operations*

Nonetheless, I am at liberty to view the text from *the standpoint of poetics*, for whatever reason.

I can speak of its *mimetic* value. For it is, after all, a perfect imitation of a set of instructions, conveying to us a kind of knowledge that transcends the content of a real set of instructions; what we get from the text is the very essence of instruction*hood* or -*ness*, a higher truth than mere servile knowledge concerning the operation of computers.

The text is extraordinarily *expressive* in its very impersonality, authorhood completely effaced in a book that has not even the humanizing "Anon." to provide a speaking voice. It is Lyotard who portrays for us, with singular clarity and force, the condition of knowledge in a postmodern, computerized society: knowledge as a commodity, very much like breakfast cereals or refrigerators.

> The old principle that the acquisition of knowledge is indissociable from the training (*Bildung*) of minds, or even of individuals, is becoming obsolete and will become ever more so. The relationship of the suppliers and users of knowledge to the knowledge they supply and use is now tending, and will increasingly tend, to assume the form already taken by the relationship of commodity producers and consumers to the commodities they produce and consume—that is, the form of value. (4)

In the IBM text, the postmodern producer is speaking to the consumer, and the effect on the reader is almost unbearably tragic, for the voice is that of the end of knowledge as we have known it.

From the *pragmatic* standpoint, the text in question is, when read properly, clearly an inadvertent condemnation of postmodernist capitalism. The fifty-seven words and the cluster of special symbols, value-laden in their guise of transparency and objectivity, are representative of the whole book from which they come, a volume that inducts beginners (with the use even of cartoon-character rebuses) into the world of Big Blue as if that were neutral territory. The effect of *IBM PC Convertible Guide to Operations* is to short-circuit political, economic, and ethical questions by presenting useful information in a maximally accessible way, very much as the dope dealer hooks unwary teenagers by feeding them narcotics-laced sweets.

There is, of course, no return from the world entered through the *IBM PC Convertible Guide to Operations*, no option to switch to the other, fruitful cybernetic empire. One thus becomes an active though unwitting partisan in a war between corporate giants, the winning of which is no less consequential than the very control of society. As Lyotard says, "Access to data is, and will continue to be, the prerogative of experts of all stripes. The ruling class is and will continue to be the class of decision makers. Even now it is no longer composed of the traditional political class, but of a composite layer of corporate leaders, high-level administrators, and the heads of major professional, labor, political, and religious organizations" (14).

Objective analysis of the passage is perhaps minimally rewarding, but nonetheless essential.

Perhaps the most obvious feature is the style, which might be characterized as choppy. The passage contains four complete sentences, which, to achieve flow, might have been combined thus:

Because DOS uses the file name to find the file on the diskette, each file on a diskette must have a different name.
In DOS, file names contain 1 to 8 characters which can be any of the following. . . .

Another, perhaps better, alternative is this:

Because DOS uses the name to find the file, each file on the diskette must have a different name containing 1 to 8 characters, which can be any of the following. . . .

The question is, however, "What would be gained and what lost by changing the style?"

Though one must not wax overly enthusiastic about what is, certainly, a very minor, even minimal, piece, nonetheless, the text does have its virtues, the most obvious and important of which is its unity of statement and tone. It is completely straightforward, simple, unmetaphoric. Even the special symbols at the end of the passage do not change the cool matter-of- factness that characterizes the piece. Thus, one feels that revising the style—as in the examples above—would tend to destroy the text's aura of naive clarity. Syntactically elaborate sentences in the example text would be as out of keeping as barroom profanity would be in a Jane Austen novel.

Under the aegis of mimetic criticism, we can legitimately consider the problems of referential discourse (Jakobson; Kinneavy 73–210), of scene (Burke, *Grammar* 127–70), of locution (Searle, *Speech Acts*), and of *logos*. With the expressive stance, we consider expressive discourse (Kinneavy 393–449) or, to use Jakobson's term, emotive discourse; agent (Burke, *Grammar* 171–226); illocution (Searle); and *ethos*. The terms associated with pragmatic criticism are persuasive discourse (Kinneavy 211–306; Burke, *Rhetoric of Motives* 49–54); conative discourse (Jakobson); identification (Burke, *Rhetoric of Mo-*

tives 55–58); perlocution (Searle); *pathos*. Terms associated with objective criticism are style, form, unity, texture, irony.

In other words, we have the following clusters of terms:

Ethos: expressive discourse, emotive discourse, agent, illocution
Pathos: persuasive discourse, conative discourse, identification, perlocution
Logos: referential discourse, scene, locution

In fact, the above schema is the rubric underlying this book.

In attempting to account for the dynamics of a text, we can privilege any one of them, interpreting *Pilgrim at Tinker Creek* ethically, as expressive discourse; *Dispatches* pathetically, as persuasive discourse; *The Right Stuff* logically, as referential discourse—or *Pilgrim at Tinker Creek* as referential, *Dispatches* as ethical, and *The Right Stuff* as pathetic.

By adding *form* to the rubric, we can begin to account for esthetic reading: immersion in a text *of any kind*. Or to put the matter another way: immersion in a text is the esthetic experience of reading. In esthetic reading, everything "adds up"; one's attention remains "endophoric"; one does not pause to consider the information or truth value of the text. Interpreting this experience is inevitably to give a formal account. Norman Holland and Aristotle were right when they said that, as Holland puts it, "one thing audiences do is try to find a unity in what they see, a central theme or meaning or idea around which the various details of the play or story come to a focus" (12). In the discussion of *The Snow Leopard* (chapter 6), I have tried to give such an account—of how the elements of *ethos* and *logos* add up, in my reading, to an esthetic whole.

The schema that Roman Jakobson developed in "Linguistics and Poetics" has become virtually a cliché, probably because it is so useful as a heuristic. Though I will not here rehearse it, I want readers to be aware that I have it in the back of my mind as I go about discussing texts.

Every text has elements of expression, information, and appeal to an audience (i.e., *ethos, logos,* and *pathos*). Or, readers can attribute elements of *ethos, pathos,* and *logos* to any text. Every text taken to be a text has *form* or *structure*.

Suppose, then, that we engage an advertising firm to construct for us a neon display, like this:

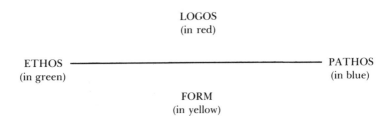

Suppose further that we associate a category of discourse with each color, like this:

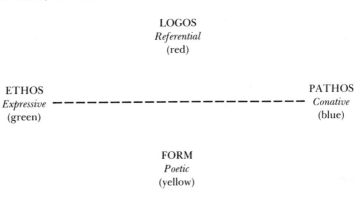

Now we add a further refinement: a rheostat, whereby one can control the brightness of each of the elements, making *logos* glow *almost* to the exclusion of *ethos, pathos,* and *form;* or turning up *pathos,* thereby dimming *ethos, logos,* and *form.*

We are now, after all, in Las Vegas! As Tom Wolfe said,

One can look at Las Vegas from a mile away on Route 91 and see no buildings, no trees, only signs. But such signs! They tower. They revolve, they oscillate, they soar in shapes before which the existing vocabulary of art history is helpless. I can only attempt to supply names—Boomerang Modern, Palette Curvilinear, Flash Gordon Ming-Alert Spiral, McDonald's Hamburger Parabola, Mint Casino Elliptical, Miami Beach Kidney. Las Vegas's sign makers work so far out beyond the frontiers of conventional art that they have no names themselves for the forms they create. ("Las Vegas" 7)

The infinitely inventive Las Vegas sign makers have constructed our neon display! But they have *not* enabled us to black any one of the elements out! Regardless of how bright one—*ethos, logos, pathos, form*—glows, the others will be perceptible if the reader attends closely.

As I manipulate the rheostat, I hope to illuminate a number of worthwhile texts.

The Rhetoric of the
"Other" Literature

CHAPTER 1
Presentational Literature

There is, first, the literature of *knowledge;* and, secondly, the literature of *power.* The function of the first is—to *teach;* the function of the second is—to *move:* the first is a rudder, the second an oar or a sail. The first speaks to the *mere* discursive understanding, the second speaks ultimately, it may happen, to the higher understanding or reason, but always *through* affections of pleasure and sympathy.
—DeQuincey, "The Literature of Knowledge and the Literature of Power"

I want the pages that follow always to be in the context of two mottoes: (1) Poetry is where you find it. (2) None of my conclusions are absolutes.

To explain the first of these, I like to give the following example. Using a public telephone not long ago, waiting for the answer to the rings, I idly read:

> —Lift receiver.
> —Listen for dial tone.
> —Deposit 20 cents.
> —Dial number.

It occurred to me that this is typical corporate language: "voiceless," flat, machinelike, dull.

A couple of days later, I received from a publisher a brightly covered book with the title *Now Poems.* Thumbing through the pages, I found a piece of verse that pleased me greatly. It was wry and ironic, but not vicious; the poet's "voice" was loud and clear; it was witty. The poem was a trifle shocking, a bit naughty, but not nasty, with its imagery of fingers in holes and coins in slots. The title was "AT&T." The poem read as follows:

1

—Lift receiver.
—Listen for dial tone.
—Deposit 20 cents.
—Dial number.

As for tentativeness: finally I am going to argue that the literature often called non-imaginative (an extremely problematic term) can be divided into two classes, which I call "discursive" and "presentational," but like the cut between imaginative and non-imaginative literature, this is not a clean distinction by which neither class has traces of the other. I will further argue that presentational literature can be divided into "narrative" and "thematic," but this is more a strategy for discovering some of the ways of texts than it is an attempt to create airtight categories.

Since about 1973, when Tom Wolfe published his manifesto on "the new journalism," a body of texts referred to most frequently as "the literature of fact" has gained the attention, if not the total respect, of the literary establishment. In the last few years, a substantial number of scholarly studies have begun to assess this literature and to place it in history, among them: Chris Anderson, *Style as Argument;* Shelley Fisher Fishkin, *From Fact to Fiction;* John Hellmann, *Fables of Fact;* John Hollowell, *Fact & Fiction;* Mas'ud Zavarzadeh, *The Mythopoeic Reality;* and though it deals with realistic fiction, Barbara Foley's *Telling the Truth* is important to the literature of fact. In 1976, the proceedings of the 1975 English Institute were published as *The Literature of Fact,* edited by Angus Fletcher.

Concomitant with this critical-theoretical interest, of course, is a significant body of new literature, beginning perhaps in 1965 with *In Cold Blood,* the first nonfiction novel to become a national best seller (though Lillian Ross's *Picture* had preceded it by a decade), and *The Kandy-Kolored Tangerine-Flake Streamline Baby,* the first monument of the new journalism. (For some obvious reasons, many of the nonfiction novels that followed *In Cold Blood* tended to be as gory as their predecessor: *The Onion Field, Blood and Money,* and Norman Mailer's masterpiece *The Executioner's Song,* among others. After all, murder and mayhem have the elements of tragedy and also lurid popular appeal.)

But works outside the nonfiction novel and the new journalism were gaining readers, if not scholarly and critical attention, new or renascent forms of literature that I call "the confessional autobiography" (e.g., Jack Henry Abbott, *In the Belly of the Beast*); the lyric in prose (e.g., Richard Selzer, "Diary of an Infidel"); and gonzo journalism (e.g., Hunter Thompson, *Fear and Loathing in Las Vegas*). A study of this extraordinarily rich body of literature is well worthwhile: (1) it has much to tell us about contemporary literate culture, (2) it gives us a new angle on poetics and rhetoric, and (3) it takes us directly into the history and politics of the literary establishment.

I will begin with a series of unsatisfactory categories labeled with equally unsatisfactory terms and ask the reader's indulgence while I limn a general outline of the subject I intend to write about in this book.

Literature

I take the field of literature to be undefined and indefinable, but knowable in a rough and ready way. E. D. Hirsch, Jr., very cleverly proposes an experiment:

I can gather a group of educated persons and set before them a series of texts paired off in groups of two. I can then ask them to write down on each text either the letter L or the letter N, standing for "literature" and "non-literature," I can choose the examples with care to exclude borderline cases, and then look confidently at the results of the experiment. After some trial and error, I can easily devise a list which produces uniform and unanimous judgments from all educated persons. (24)

On the other hand, he says, he could just as easily produce a list that would arouse debate, one including letters by canonical authors, some histories, biographies, certain political speeches, and even a number of scientific works (25).

Propounding a valid formal definition of literature is as fruitless an endeavor as attempting to give rules, rather than rules of thumb, for the personal essay or naturalistic novel. It is generally accepted that there are such categories; readers can in most cases agree which texts belong in a category; but listing the salient differentiae, so that all members of the class will be included and no nonmembers, is the sort of futile exercise that sometimes makes scholars outside the field of literary studies wonder about the epistemologies, methods, and goals of those inside the field.

Yet a loose understanding of what is and what is not literature does prevail. Before the eighteenth century, literature consisted of texts that had worth or quality and permanence or the prospect thereof, and this view persists to a certain extent now. Both polemically and ironically, Hirsch puts the matter this way: "Literature includes any text worthy to be taught to students by teachers of literature, when these texts are not being taught to students in other departments of a school or university" (34).

However, both the popular conception of literature and the tacit understanding of it among scholars makes "imaginative" works central and other texts peripheral. If you ask your lawyer, accountant, or physician to give you examples of literature, the response will not be *The Voyage of the Beagle* or "Self-Reliance," but *Hamlet* or "Ode on a Grecian Urn." Furthermore, if you look at the course offerings in English departments and at the texts that the members of those departments choose to teach, you will find in most cases that non-imaginative literature occupies little space, if any, and that on the fringes.

According to René Wellek, the tendency to associate the term "literature" with fiction or imaginative writings is a comparatively recent development, beginning in the eighteenth century with the invention of the term "aesthetic" by Baumgarten in 1735 and culminating in the distinction among the beautiful, the true, the good, and the useful in Kant's 1790 *Critique of Judgment* (Wellek 20–21).

Whatever the history, by the twentieth century, literature as understood in the academy and among literary scholars included fictional narrative, poetry, and drama and pretty much excluded historical narrative (including autobiography and biography) and all forms of exposition, argumentation, and persuasion, except as these genres were part of a fiction, as in the philosophical or muckraking novel.

In the twentieth century, successive purges have "purified" literature, the dross of "fact" being smelted off to leave the pure gold of imagination: poetry, prose fiction, and drama. Two monuments of literary theory represent the current-traditional view of what constitutes a literature worthy of study: Wellek and Warren's *Theory of Literature* and Northrop Frye's *The Anatomy of Criticism.*

Undoubtedly Wellek and Warren were reacting to crisis when, in 1942, they proposed to construct a theory of literature. Positivism was skeptical of value questions; behaviorism had reduced human action to mere motion; science was becoming ever more triumphant in both its theoretical and applied aspects. In the meantime, the literary scholar was going on with his tatting and crewelwork, a quaint soul for whom the university must provide a niche and a subsistence wage since it is the function of the institution of higher learning not only to advance knowledge, but also to preserve the tradition.

"The problem," said Wellek and Warren, "is one of how, intellectually, to deal with art, and with literary art specifically" (16). Assuring us that "literary scholarship has its own valid methods which are not always those of the natural sciences but are nevertheless intellectual methods" (16), they solve the problem by reducing the object of study to language: "Language is the material of literature as stone or bronze is of sculpture, paints of pictures, or sounds of music. But one should realize that language is not mere inert matter like stone but is itself a creation of man and is thus charged with the cultural heritage of a group" (22). Then they move one step further, to say that literature is its own truth: "art is substantively beautiful and adjectivally true (i.e., doesn't conflict with truth)" (34). Using Susanne K. Langer's well-known distinction, Wellek and Warren tell us that the truth in literature is presentational (i.e., intuitive, emotional), not discursive (amenable to propositional explanation, as in philosophy).

What Wellek and Warren lead up to but do not say is that presentational texts are literature, whereas discursive texts are not.

The Anatomy of Criticism devalued non-imaginative literature even further. "For Frye," says Frank Lentricchia, "actual history can be nothing but a theater of dehumanization, a place of bondage and torture" (26), from which literature provides an escape. As Frye says,

In literature, questions of fact or truth are subordinated to the primary literary aim of producing a structure of words for its own sake, and the sign-values of symbols are subordinated to their importance as a structure of interconnected motifs. Wherever we have an autonomous verbal structure of this kind, we have literature. Wherever this autonomous structure is lacking, we have language, words used instrumentally to help human consciousness do or understand something else. (74)

And *that* pretty much banishes from the realm of literature many of the texts that will concern us throughout the pages of this book: not only straight reportage as in *Hiroshima*, but such fringe specimens as *The Executioner's Song*.

In his "classic" essay "The New Journalism," Tom Wolfe has given vital testimony to the false dichotomy: "pure" imaginative literature and "servile" non-imaginative texts. He speaks of the time and effort that Jimmy Breslin and other journalists put into the gathering of background information, but

Literary people were oblivious to this side of the New Journalism, because it is one of the unconscious assumptions of modern criticism that the raw material is simply "there." It is the "given." The idea is: Given such-and-such a body of material, what has the artist done with it? The crucial part that reporting plays in all story-telling, whether in novels, films, or non-fiction, is something that is not so much ignored as simply not comprehended. The modern notion of art is an essentially religious or magical one in which the artist is viewed as a holy beast who in some way, big or small, receives flashes from the godhead, which is known as creativity. The material is merely his clay, his palette. . . . Even the obvious relationship between reporting and the major novels— one has only to think of Balzac, Dickens, Gogol, Tolstoy, Dostoyevsky, and, in fact, Joyce—is something that literary historians deal with only in a biographical sense. It took the New Journalism to bring this strange matter of reporting into the foreground. (14)

In the first chapter of *Literary Theory: An Introduction,* Terry Eagleton systematically debunks definitions of literature that rely on the imaginative–non-imaginative distinction (1–2), formalist criteria (2–7), and the supposedly non-pragmatic nature of literary texts (7–10). He arrives at a conclusion to which I subscribe (and which this book will elaborate):

Anything can be literature, and anything which is regarded as unalterably and unquestionably literature—Shakespeare, for example—can cease to be literature. Any belief that the study of literature is the study of a stable, well-definable entity, as entomology is the study of insects, can be abandoned as a chimera. Some kinds of fiction are literature and some are not; some literature is fictional and some is not; some literature is verbally self-regarding, while some highly-wrought rhetoric is not literature. Literature, in the sense of a set of works of assured and unalterable value, distinguished by certain shared inherent properties, does not exist. (10–11)

I take the latitudinarian, somewhat old-fashioned view of literature as texts that (1) communities of readers value for their intrinsic worth[1] and (2) have staying power or appear likely to have it.

---

[1] I am not claiming that any work of literature has universal, eternal, inherent worth; readers do, however, attribute value to works.

"Non-Imaginative" Literature

On the one hand, perhaps we could achieve universal agreement that by my loose definition Macaulay's *History of England from the Accession of James the Second* and *Areopagitica* are literature, but that they are not "imaginative literature" as that term is usually thought of. On the other hand, the house would undoubtedly divide over the question of whether or not *In Cold Blood* and "Diary of an Infidel," by Richard Selzer, are imaginative literature.

It may bespeak a certain pusillanimousness, but I will skirt the issue of what reality is or how it is perceived and will turn to Coleridge's distinction between the primary and the secondary imagination, which certainly is part of the historical reason for the devaluation of non-imaginative literature.

The primary imagination is a sort of camera that copies reality. The secondary imagination is re-creative and vital:

> The primary *imagination* I hold to be the living Power and prime Agent of all human Perception, and as a repetition in the finite mind of the eternal act of creation in the infinite *I am.* The secondary I consider as an echo of the former, co-existing with the conscious will, yet still as identical with the primary in the *kind* of its agency, and differing only in *degree,* and in the *mode* of its operation. It dissolves, diffuses, dissipates, in order to re-create; or where this process is rendered impossible, yet still at all events it struggles to idealize and to unify. It is essentially *vital,* even as all objects (*as* objects) are essentially fixed and dead. (I, 304)

The distinction between the *copy* produced by the primary imagination and the *imitation* produced by the secondary imagination tallies with Wellek and Warren's shibboleth that "art is substantively beautiful and adjectivally true (i.e., doesn't conflict with truth)" and Frye's conviction that "wherever we have an autonomous verbal structure . . . we have literature."

Imaginative literature, then, is of a higher order than non-imaginative, for it represents true creativity, and we look to it not for information about the world or even, as a matter of fact, for moral wisdom "because the object in view, as an *immediate* object, belongs to the moral philosopher, and would be pursued, not only more appropriately, but in my opinion with far greater probability of success, in sermons or moral essays, than in an elevated poem" (Coleridge II:130). The immediate end of poetry is pleasure, not truth, but, paradoxically, the truth that one gains from poetry is a psychological or epistemological insight, for the symbols of art are not servile, but represent "the mind perceiving its own self in relation to nature" (Engell and Bate lxxxiii).

For the unavoidably pejorative term "non-imaginative literature," we might substitute the equally pejorative "non-creative" (i.e., resulting from primary imagination). In any case, the following pages will deal with non-imaginative, non-creative literature.

Presentational Literature

Both of DeQuincey's essays "The Literature of Knowledge and the Literature of Power" and "Levana and Our Ladies of Sorrow" are non-imaginative literature, yet they are of different orders. I will call the former "discursive" and the latter "presentational," terms that I hope to rehabilitate.

In a rough-and-ready way, we can differentiate these two essays, and I think that intuitively readers would put them in separate categories. To use DeQuincey's happy terminology, "The Literature of Knowledge and the Literature of Power" belongs to the literature of knowledge, while "Levana" is an example of the literature of power.

In "Literature," DeQuincey tells us that the one essential element of literature is its universality, its "relation to a general and common interest of man, so that what applies only to a local, or professional, or merely personal interest, even though presenting itself in the shape of a book, will not belong to literature." Of the class literature there are two categories: those works which teach and those works which move, the literatures of knowledge and power. "The first speaks to the *mere* discursive understanding; the second speaks ultimately, it may happen, to the higher understanding or reason, but always *through* affections of pleasure and sympathy." DeQuincey clinches his argument with this wonderful, sophistic comparison: "What do you learn from *Paradise Lost?* Nothing at all. What do you learn from a cookery book? Something new, something that you did not know before, in every paragraph." In particular, the discursiveness of the literature of knowledge makes it paraphrasable. It is important to note that *one can argue for or against the thesis of the essay.*

The characteristic of the literature of power is its total uniqueness:

Human works of immortal beauty and works of nature in one respect stand on the same footing: they never absolutely repeat each other, never approach so near as not to differ; and they differ not as better and worse, or simply by more and less; they differ by indecipherable and incommunicable differences that cannot be caught by mimicries, that cannot be reflected in the mirror of copies, that cannot become ponderable in the scales of vulgar comparison. (333–34)

"Levana," of course, is not everyone's favorite example of literature, but by our definition, it clearly *is* literature, having intrinsic worth, at least for many readers over the long haul, and, for whatever reason, staying power. The gist of the essay summarized provides no basis for argument: In allegorizing the grief he experienced when he was sent off to Eton, DeQuincey makes Levana represent the goddess of childhood passions with her three Ladies, of Tears, of Sighs, and of Darkness. The only argument provided by "Levana" concerns its own status as art.

To be sure, DeQuincey was not an original or systematic thinker as was Coleridge, but in "The Literature of Knowledge and the Literature of Power," he provides an apposite and lucid statement of an idea that had been in the air since classical times. (For instance, the *Phaedrus* is an argument in favor of both passion and uniqueness as opposed to cool, prudent reason.)

In the next few pages, I would like to pursue that idea from three perspectives: Susanne Langer's distinction between discursive and presentational symbolism; the psychologist Endel Tulving's characterization of "semantic" and "episodic" memory; and Kenneth Burke's explanation of "lyric."

Langer's Discursive and Presentational Symbolism

In *Philosophy in a New Key*, which derives from the work of Ernst Cassirer, Susanne Langer says that verbal symbolism is discursive:

[A]ll language has a form which requires us to string out our ideas even though their objects rest one within the other; as pieces of clothing that are actually worn one over the other have to be strung side by side on the clotheslines. This property of verbal symbolism is known as *discursiveness;* by reason of it, only thoughts which can be arranged in this peculiar order can be spoken at all; any idea which does not lend itself to this "projection" is ineffable, incommunicable by means of words. (77)

Langer goes on, almost passionately, to debunk the positivists, who were claiming that the *only* knowledge is discursive—poetry, music, and the visual and plastic arts being merely symptoms of subjective experience and thus the subject matter of psychology, not of semantics (81). From the arts, we derive meanings that philosophers have been unwilling to consider—"intuition," "deeper meaning," "artistic truth," and so forth (84)—conveyed by presentational symbolism, of which the most highly developed form is music (93).

However, texts—poems, stories, essays—have a presentational function in their totality.[2]

> The meanings given through language are successively understood, and gathered into a whole by the process called discourse; the meanings of all other symbolic elements that compose a larger, articulate symbol are understood only through the meaning of the whole, through their relations with the total structure. Their very functioning as symbols depends on the fact that they are involved in a simultaneous, integral presentation. This kind of semantic may be called "presentational symbolism," to characterize its essential distinction from discursive symbolism, or "language" proper. (89)

As Howard Gardner (50–52), among others, points out, Langer's distinction is problematic and has been roundly criticized. Langer provides few examples, and her definitions are hazy, yet she has the indirect support of literary theorists such as Allen Tate, who, in "Literature as Knowledge" (first published in 1941), says, "We must return to, we must never leave, the poem itself. Its 'interest' value is a cognitive one; it is sufficient that here, in the poem, we get knowledge of a whole object. . . . However we may see the completeness of poetry, it is a problem less to be solved than, in its full import, to be preserved" (941).

In sum, we have reached the position that the meaning and value of a poem are in its autonomous totality, not in its discursive (and servile) function. Literary texts that have the taint of discursiveness are valued less highly than "pure" literature. We have also retrieved the term "presentational," the dialectic of which reveals the nature

---

[2] It would be interesting to claim or demonstrate that *Philosophy in a New Key* influenced Wellek and Warren in *Theory of Literature*, but, unfortunately, both were first published in 1942, a historical fact significant enough to mark the beginning of an era. In the 1956 edition of *Theory*, Wellek and Warren cite Langer and make the discursive-presentational distinction.

of a group of non-imaginative literary texts. Furthermore, we cling to the distinction suggested by two groups of terms:

primary imagination	secondary imagination
literature of knowledge	literature of power
discursive symbolism	presentational symbolism

Tulving's Semantic and Episodic Memory

It turns out also that standard psychological theory supports the kind of distinction made by DeQuincey and Langer. In 1972, Endel Tulving proposed that memory has two components, the *semantic* (or "verbal") and the *episodic*. Semantic memory is "a mental thesaurus, organized knowledge a person possesses about words and other verbal symbols, their meanings and referents, about relations among them, about rules, formulas, and algorithms for the manipulation of these symbols, concepts, and relations" (386).

Episodic memory

1. "receives and stores information about temporally dated episodes or events";
2. also receives and stores temporal-spatial relationships among these events;
3. can store events solely in terms of perceptible properties or attributes;
4. always stores in terms of the events' "autobiographical reference to the already existing contents" of episodic memory. (385–86)

For example,

Semantic Knowledge

1. "I remember that the chemical formula for common table salt is NaCl."
2. "I know that summers are usually quite hot in Katmandu."
3. "I know that the name of the month that follows June is July, if we consider them in the order in which they occur in the calendar, or March, if we consider them in alphabetical order."

Episodic Knowledge

1. "I remember seeing a flash of light a short while ago, followed by a loud sound a few seconds later."
2. "Last year, while on my summer vacation, I met a retired sea captain who knew more jokes than any other person I have ever met."
3. "I remember that I have an appointment with a student at 9:30 tomorrow morning." (386–87)

Tulving's semantic knowledge and Langer's discursive symbolism square with one another so nicely as to need no comment, but episodic knowledge and presentational symbolism are not obviously synonymous, even in a rough way. If, however, we find the central argument that Langer and Tulving advance, we will have made a gain in the attempt to delineate certain fields of literature.

Langer is saying something like this: some semantic intentions are expressible only through poems, a self-evident tautological thesis. And Tulving, if we boil his argument down to its essentials, is saying, "Much of what we know is personal, autobiographical, meshed inextricably with our souls and psyches, and is expressible through narrative."

Poems and stories, then, are representations of much of our knowledge. In the next section of this chapter, we will deal with the "poem," and with the story in its various guises throughout the book.

We now can bring the discussion up to date by aligning terms once more:

primary imagination	secondary imagination
literature of knowledge	literature of power
discursive symbolism	presentational symbolism
semantic knowledge	*episodic knowledge*

Kenneth Burke and the Lyric

As early as 1941, Kenneth Burke was making counterstatements to the views represented by Wellek and Warren, Langer, and Tate insofar as these theorists claimed autonomy for poems. In *The Philosophy of Literary Form,* Burke says that poetry, or any verbal act, is to be considered as "symbolic action." But though I must use this term, I object strenuously to having the general perspective labeled as "symbolism." I recognize that people like to label, that labeling *comforts* them by *getting things placed*. But I object to "symbolism" as a label because it suggests too close a link with a particular school of poetry, the Symbolist Movement, and usually implies the unreality of the world in which we live, as though nothing could be what it is, but must always be something else. (8–9)

In one of his most apt and memorable phrases, Burke said that the symbolic act is the *dancing of an attitude* (9).

Though the poem is undoubtedly a symbol system, and thus is to be analyzed structurally, it is also an *action* (as opposed to mere physical motion) and thus is to be analyzed in terms of what Burke later was to call "dramatism," but which in 1941 amounted to the heresy of denying the work's autonomy. In the context of the 1940's, Burke was an odd bird indeed, talking about literature in ways that one might use to gossip about one's neighbors, as if literature were part of the quotidian:

I know of a man who, going to a dentist, was proud of the calmness with which he took his punishment. But after the session was ended, the dentist said to him: "I observe that you were very much afraid of me. For I have noted that, when patients are frightened, their saliva becomes thicker, more sticky. And yours was exceptionally so." Which would indicate that, while the man in the dentist's chair was "dancing an attitude of calmness" on the public level, as a social façade, on the purely bodily or biological level his salivary glands were "dancing his true attitude." (*Philosophy* 11)

From Kenneth Burke, we derive the notion that as a speech act, the lyric is an expression of attitude, a special kind of text that shifts attention toward the addresser. Regardless of what the lyric is "about," we are more interested in the poet's attitude than in the ostensible subject matter, and an attitude is the preparation for an act, a state of mind that may or may not lead to an act (*Grammar* 20). "It may be either an incipient act or the substitute for an act" (*Grammar* 476). A citizen who "on perfectly rational grounds" rejects the powers that be might compose poems "enacting his attitude of rejection" (*Philosophy* 11).

In "The Anaesthetic Revelation of Herone Liddel," the last tale in *The Complete White Oxen*, Burke makes his definitive statement concerning attitude:

An *attitude* towards a body of topics has a unifying force. In effect its unitary nature as a response "sums up" the conglomerate of particulars towards which the attitude is directed.

Attitudes, in this respect, are a kind of censorial entitling, reduced to terms of behaviour. They are an implicit charade, a way of "acting out" a situation. Or they are like a highly generalized term of classification, a broad logical category—for in effect they classify under one head all the many different particular situations that call forth the same attitude. (290)

As Burke himself has stated (during a 1977 conference at the University of Southern California), the notion of attitude is closely related to the speech act theorists' *illocution* and, in fact, solves one problem that Mary Louise Pratt attempts to deal with in her illuminating study, *Toward a Speech Act Theory of Literary Discourse*, that of applying sentence-bound speech act theory to whole discourses. In the next chapter, we will deal with these problems.

In the "pure" narrative, the dramatistic ratio is that of scene-act—as Aristotle said, "Tragedy is essentially an imitation not of persons but of action and life, of happiness and misery. All human happiness or misery takes the form of action; the end for which we live is a certain kind of activity, not a quality." The lyric ratio, however, is that of scene-agent, and a subtle, but very important, shift has taken place, for now the addresser, the poet, enters.

We can analyze both drama and lyric from the standpoint of language in general or of poetics in particular. As instances of language in general, every literary work must finally be dealt with "as the product of a citizen and taxpayer, subject to various social embarrassments, physical ills, and mental aberrations" ("Poetics in Particular" 38). In such a case, "scene" means the world in which the taxpayer exists; and "act" means what this taxpayer, as poet, did in regard to that world; "agent" implies not a doing, but, in Burke's own language, the poet who sets forth "the summation or culmination of action, transcending overt action by *symbolically* encompassing its end" (*Grammar* 245).

In drama there is the intense internal debate prior to the moment of decision. Upon the outcome of this debate depends the course of history. But from the lyric point of view, the state of arrest is itself an end-product, a resolution of previous action rather than a preparation for subsequent action (though of course while life is still in progress any culminating stage is but *pro tempore*, and can also be the beginning of a new development). (*Grammar* 245)

Thus, Burke distinguishes drama and lyric. Presentational texts are lyrical. It is now our purpose to argue that insofar as narrative texts have elements of lyric, they are presentational.

Narrative and Thematic Texts

Paradoxically, I am now going to claim that in presentational literature, both narrative and "thematic" works are lyrical. I derive the term "thematic" from Northrop Frye, who, in "Myth, Fiction, and Displacement," divides literary works into two classes: fictional and thematic. For obvious reasons, I have changed "fictional" to "narrative," and when Frye explains his terms, one feels that he would be amenable to the switch: "[Fiction] comprises works of literature with internal characters, and includes novels, plays, narrative poetry, folk tales, and *everything that tells a story*. In thematic literature the author and the reader are the only characters involved: this division includes most lyrics, essays, didactic poetry and oratory" (my emphasis) (21).

If presentational literature is lyrical, how can it at the same time be narrative? (The chapter on narrative will deal with the problem of differentiating history and fiction. It is enough at present to establish the presentational.) Reading, say, a Hardy novel, the sequence of actions engages us, the series of events and scenes that constitute the story, but after having finished the work, our possession of it is a gestalt, not a series. We have the theme, the incidents of the story "discontinuous, detached from one another and regrouped in a new way" (23), consisting of three elements: the subject, which can usually be expressed in a summary; the allegorical value, which, for example, makes Hamlet into the personification of indecision; and "*mythos* or plot examined as a simultaneous unity" (24).

The intuitive rightness of Frye's account of reading is verified by psychological studies. Teun A. van Dijk's widely known work, for instance, has readers seeking a *macroproposition* that controls the whole text and allows them to construct a *semantic macrostructure*, which is not the same as the formal superstructure of the text (42). The best image of the macrostructure is a tree diagram with the macroproposition as the superordinate node, representing the coherence that the reader derives from (or constructs for) the text; the best image for the superstructure is an outline representing the surface arrangement of parts. (As we shall see, Hayden White differentiates chronicle and history on the basis of the latter's thematization.)

After the fact of reading, then, the narrative, as it lives in memory, is thematic, just as the lyric is. If the scene-agent ratio prevails, the work is also lyrical. Thus, *The Armies of the Night*—essentially Norman Mailer's confession, not a history of the march on the Pentagon—is a markedly lyrical work whereas *Hiroshima* is just as markedly unlyrical. On the other hand, texts such as lyric poems frequently contain traces of narrative. Is it not the case that terms such as "lyric," "expository," "persuasive," "narrative," and "descriptive" apply to semantic intentions, not to texts viewed as formal structures?

Features of Presentational Texts

Presentational texts are often marked by features that are less frequent in discursive texts, recessive characteristics that spill over the boundaries of the presentational into the discursive, but that tend to be less dense in that hemisphere. (1) Presentational works are often densely textured and hence reified. (2) The author frequently uses fictional devices such as invented dialogue. The author and the reader enter a special interpretive contract, sanctioning the devices named above and others, but since this book concerns the writer-reader contract, I will here discuss only texture and invented dialogue.

Texture

In the first chapter of *Toward a Speech Act Theory of Literature*, Mary Louise Pratt definitively explained "The 'Poetic Language' Fallacy." Throughout all of the literature on stylistics produced in this century, poeticians and other theorists have failed to show that the features they identify in poetic language are not also a part of "ordinary language." " 'Nonpoetic' could be specified variously as 'practical,' 'utilitarian,' 'spoken,' 'prosaic,' 'scientific,' 'everyday,' 'communicative,' 'referential,' or any combination of these without in the least disturbing the notion of what 'poetic' was" (5–6).

I will, of course, not argue that there is a poetic language, but I will demonstrate the obvious: that language can be more or less *textured,* meaning simply that the phonemic, graphemic, syntactic, and semantic systems vary in their "transparency."

In "ordinary" reading, subvocalization is minimal, though it increases for everyone with the difficulty of the text, and everyone finds some texts difficult (Taylor and Taylor 209–14). In some cases, even with highly skilled readers, subvocalization becomes outright vocalization, reading aloud in the attempt to gain meaning. The increase in subvocalization is a paradoxical tradeoff: the more the reader is aware of the language system itself—in this case, the so-called graphophonic correspondence—the less he or she gains in the way of meaning, yet pronouncing aloud brings two senses to bear on the task of building the meaning, and the vocalization brings a richer supply of blood to Broca's area of the brain.

As poets have always known, it is possible to increase the difficulty of a text—i.e., decrease its readability or accessibility—by creating features that call attention to the language system, namely, rhyme and alliteration. Insofar as attention is diverted from meaning to sound, reading is more difficult.

Whether or not the following pairs of sentences have exactly the same meanings, they certainly have the same propositional content. (See Kintsch, *The Representation of Meaning in Memory*.)

1. The horse raced around the track dropped dead.
1a. The horse that was raced around the track dropped dead.

2. That Harry told Larry that Mary said Barry is odd is strange.
2a. It is strange that Harry told Larry that Mary said Barry is odd.

3. Whatever they couldn't buy at the country store located at the crossroads five miles from town the family did without.
3a. The family did without whatever they couldn't buy at the country store located at the crossroads five miles from town.

Syntax, then, can make sentences more or less accessible, and the less accessible they are, the more the text is reified, just as in the case of the graphophonic system.

Finally, if a reader takes a given text to be a poem, he or she uses different interpretive strategies than would be the case with a nonpoetic text. (In understanding these strategies, Philip Wheelwright's "The Logical and the Translogical" is most useful.) The rose in Yeats' and Waller's poems is quite different from the rose in the *Sunset Book of Gardening*, the poetic rose gaining its essential significance as a symbol from the context in which it occurs.

Since I have alluded to two essays by DeQuincey, I will briefly use one of them as a case in point regarding texture. Happily for my purposes, "Levana" begins with an *alliteration:*

*O*ftentimes at *O*xford I saw Levana in my dreams. I knew her by her Roman symbols. Who is Levana? Reader, that do not pretend to have leisure for very much scholarship, you will not be angry with me for telling you.

Now follows a long sentence, baroque in its *syntactic* intricacy:

Levana was the Roman goddess that performed for the newborn infant the earliest office of ennobling kindness—typical, by its mode, of that grandeur which belongs to man everywhere and of that benignity in powers invisible which even in pagan worlds sometimes descends to sustain it.

Depending from the adjective "typical" are three prepositional phrases (*by its mode, of that grandeur,* and *of that benignity*), the second and third of which are modified by adjective clauses (*which belongs to man everywhere* and *which even in pagan worlds sometimes descends to sustain it*). As a nice counterpoint to "kindness—typical," we find "powers invisible."

If the reader has, by this time, taken the essay to be poetic (in the broad sense), then he or she has begun to search for the contextual meaning of Levana, which will derive from the text and will either contradict or transcend the "dictionary" definition that DeQuincey provides in the first paragraph. By the end of the essay, Levana has become the symbol of the tragedy of childhood, not its hope.

Fictional Devices

In *Fact & Fiction: The New Journalism and the Nonfiction Novel,* John Hollowell gives an apposite and useful summary of the fictional devices that characterize the genres he discusses. First is *dramatic scene,* which is, in Hollowell's paraphrase of Henry James, "*scenic* depiction rather than historical summary" (26). For examples, one can turn almost at random to the works that fall under the heading "literature of fact." Here is the first paragraph of *Friendly Fire,* C. D. B. Bryan's gripping documentary account of one family's response to the death of their son in Vietnam:

September 3, 1969, his last night of leave, Michael Eugene Mullen worked until ten o'clock on his family's 120-acre farm five miles west of La Porte

City in Black Hawk County, Iowa. He remained down in the lower 80 acres upon his father's old plum-red Farmall H-series tractor ripping out brush and dead trees, bulldozing the trash into the dry streambed of Miller's Creek, clearing and filling in the land so it could be used as pasture again. (11)

The convention is clearly that of fiction, the author, in effect, signaling to the reader that in the course of the narrative Michael Mullen will gradually become known in detail (will develop as a character). In Northrop Frye's terminology, the movement is endophoric, directing the reader's attention inward to the narrative for information rather than outward.

The second technique that Hollowell discusses is the tendency of both fiction and the literature of fact toward *recording dialogue in full* (27), rather than quoting only brief salient patches of dialogue and summarizing the gist of the remarks.

The third "novelistic" technique is the use of what Tom Wolfe calls *status details*, "the everyday gestures, habits, manners, customs, styles of furniture, clothing, decoration . . . by which [people] experience their position in the world" (*The New Journalism* 32). For example, details of scene and character that would be irrelevant and out of keeping in a scholarly biography are the very stuff of Mailer's story of Gary Gilmore (*Executioner's Song*). After Gilmore killed his first victim, he and his girlfriend's sister spent the night at a Holiday Inn. The chapter "The Motel Room" begins with almost two pages of status detail.

> At the far end of the bedroom, to one side of the far wall, was the only window and it looked out over the swimming pool. . . . On either side hung drapes made of a green-blue synthetic fabric, and they were drawn apart by white vertical cords that passed around milk-colored plastic pulleys. . . . On the door frame of the bathroom was a switch that in the dark glowed like a squared-off fluorescent nipple. . . . The toilet paper from the toilet-paper holder on the wall to the left of the toilet seat was soft and very absorbent, and would stick to the anus. (232–33)

Needless to say, the nonfiction novel has the freedom to adopt *narrative points of view* that would be illegitimate in "straight" journalism and to use *interior monologue* (28–30). In "Author's Note to Fame and Obscurity," Gay Talese claims that he asks his subjects for their thoughts and thus gives the reader documented interior monologue, as in the following brief scene from *The Kingdom and the Power:*

Seated behind his big desk in the middle of the newsroom, Rosenthal momentarily looked up from the stories that he was reading and gazed around the room at the distant rows of desks, the reporters typing, talking among themselves, sometimes looking at him in a way he suspected was hostile—*they must despise me,* he thought, being both irritated and saddened by the possibility, *they must really hate my guts.* (353)

However, within the nonfiction novel, interior monologue is taken to be not factual reporting, but interpretation and speculation by the author and hence not in violation of the tacit conventions upon which the writer and reader agree. In Wambaugh's *The Onion Field,* Jimmy Smith is in a movie with a girl.

There was no time to be cool, thought Jimmy, and dropped his hand on Linda's hot little thigh the moment she sat. She didn't object and in fact moved down a little and sighed. Jimmy was on fire at once, reaching under her dress just as Pat came back with two boxes of popcorn and a handful of candy bars, but Jimmy's throat was so dry and constricted from Linda's presence, he couldn't swallow his popcorn without choking. Pat was by then too suspicious to go back up the aisle for sodas when he suggested it. (87)

Finally, Hollowell lists *composite characterization,* "a person who represents a whole class of subjects" (30)—such as "Raymond," whom Tom Wolfe depicts at length, "not because he is a typical Las Vegas tourist, although he has some typical symptoms, but because he is a good example of the marvelous impact Las Vegas has on the senses" ("Las Vegas (What?)" 4).

Since I will discuss *The Executioner's Song* later, I will at this point merely allude to it as an example of how fiction can be used in presentational texts. The 1,050 pages of the book contain detailed accounts of trysts, family reunions, conversations with neighbors, idle chitchat—in short all of the kinds of talk that people do over a nine-month period (the time span of the book). The writer has a choice: to create a historical biography, such as Fawn Brodie's marvelous *Thomas Jefferson,* with its scrupulous distinction between "factual" material and authorial interpretation, or a "fictionalized" biography such as *The Executioner's Song,* with its obviously invented dialogue and mind reading by an omniscient author. Both sorts of works have their value, but they invite readers to approach them differently. In the following from *The Executioner's Song,* Gary Gilmore and Nicole Baker meet for the first time: "Nicole made a pretense of ignoring the new fellow, but there was something about him. When their eyes met, he looked at her and said, 'I know you.' Nicole didn't say anything in reply. For a split second, something flashed in her mind but then she thought, No, I've never met him before, I know that. Maybe I know him from another time" (73).

Of course, I am only reiterating the obvious: the non-fiction novel is a novel that uses historical fact as its superstructure and much of its substance. (It is, however, a different genre from the historical novel as practiced by, for instance, Irving Stone, a distinction that we will get to in due time.)

A Polemical Summary

In 1938, Louise Rosenblatt's *Literature as Exploration* was published, and in 1968 and 1976 second and third editions appeared. This work was prescient, anticipating the issues that reader-response criticism (as represented in, for instance, *Reader-Response Criticism,* edited by Jane Tompkins, 1980) and deconstruction were to popularize decades later, but totally ignored by the literary establishment because, one suspects, it was addressed to grade-school and secondary teachers and was thus taintedly educationist. Also largely ignored was Rosenblatt's *The Reader, the Text, the Poem: The Transactional Theory of the Literary Work* (1978), a statement of the theory underlying her earlier volume.

The third chapter of *The Reader,* "Efferent and Aesthetic Reading," argues for a transactional theory of literature. In efferent[3] reading attention is directed toward what one will carry away—namely toward information. (As we shall see, Kenneth Burke differentiates the psychology of information and the psychology of form in reading.) "In aesthetic reading, in contrast, the reader's primary concern is with what happens *during* the actual reading event" (24). Obviously, the reader consciously or unconsciously determines the nature of the reading act—whether it is efferent or aesthetic. Anyone can read—and many people, I suspect, do read—the writing on cornflake boxes esthetically. However, for most of the readers

---

[3] From the Latin *effere* "to carry away."

of this book, under most circumstances, cornflake boxes have less *potentiality* than, for example, a poem by Yeats.[4]

In the sections preceding this one, I have outlined a few of the elements of potentiality: texture and fictional devices. As the discussion progresses, other possibilities will emerge. For example, I. A. Richards' famous *mnemonic irrelevancies*— "misleading effects of the reader's being reminded of some personal scene or adventure, erratic associations, the interference of emotional reverberations from a past which may have nothing to do with the poem" (13)— are idiosyncratic potentialities that every reader experiences. But if the poem triggers it, how can a "mnemonic irrelevance" be irrelevant and "have nothing to do with the poem"? In the first chapter of *Literature as Exploration*, Rosenblatt commonsensically argues that readers make sense of texts in two ways, in personal and in universal terms, which is to say that I must use the terms, norms, and values of my community if I am to translate my personal reaction so that it will be meaningful and "count" for the members of that community. My rhetoric must be appropriate and cogent.

In the chapters that follow, I have attempted to use appropriate, cogent rhetoric to revalue a body of texts that current-traditional literary theories devalue.

Of the 900 or so sessions held during the 1988 meeting of the Modern Language Association of America, only fifteen are listed directly under "Nonfictional Prose." This imbalance is characteristic of the literary professionals who gather every year between Christmas and New Year's Eve to discuss their concerns, exchange ideas, and drink the potables and eat the canapes supplied by publishers. The virtually monomaniacal commitment to the "imaginative" and avoidance of the "non-imaginative" is a large factor in the alienation of the literary establishment from the educated reading public. Annie Dillard, Peter Matthiessen, Richard Selzer, even Joan Didion as essayist—these authors of the common-place, read and admired by those for whom Litspeak[5] is a foreign language, are barely in the

[4] Rosenblatt says, "And a Rod McKuen text offers less potentiality than a Yeats text" (34)—a statement that propels us into the realm of absolute values. If Rosenblatt were willing to rephrase, we might not argue with her: "For given communities of readers, a Rod McKuen text offers less potentiality than a Yeats text."

[5] The term is from Gerald Graff, "Jargonorama: What We Talk About When We Talk About Lit," *Voice Literary Supplement*, January/February 1989: 22–23, 26. Graff says, "The difficulties students have with the humanities derive not from the status level of the texts, but from the special way texts of any level are read and discussed in academic institutions" (23).

contemporary canon. Thus, the establishment isolates itself from its "culturally literate" constituency, having less and less to say to nonprofessional readers.

Furthermore, the aberrant view of literature that prevails within the literary establishment contributes to one of the great academic disgraces: the scandalous situation in freshman composition and other "non-imaginative" writing courses. My colleagues in the English department at the University of Southern California place great value on our undergraduate "creative" writing courses; only recognized masters (such as my colleagues Tom Boyle and David St. John) are qualified to teach these classes (which are dedicated to producing "imaginative" texts), but the department assigns advanced composition to whichever graduate student needs support and has deserted freshman composition altogether (for these courses produce *un*imaginative texts). Those who contributed to the wistfully titled *Composition and Literature: Bridging the Gap* (Horner)[6] should look toward reunifying the canon as one of the most important moves in building the bridge.

In other words, I have both theoretical-historical and political reasons for my redefinition of literature as "texts that (1) communities of readers value for their intrinsic worth and (2) have staying power or appear likely to have it."

Readers' experiences with texts, literary doctrine, and psychological theory validate the discursive-presentational distinction, but there are compelling political reasons for the split. "Imaginative literature" and "the literature of fact" contain both discursive and presentational texts. ("Essay on Man" and "Essay on Criticism" are—or can legitimately be taken as—discursive, and yet both are securely part of the canon of imaginative literature.) That being the case, the distinction between "imaginative" and "non-imaginative" literature becomes insignificant since presentational texts, whatever their category in the MLA program, invite esthetic reading, and once again current-traditional literary ideology is undermined.

I am not at all certain that I can separate my personal tastes from my ideologies; I even suspect that one implies the other, which is to say that scrutiny of my literary tastes will reveal my ideologies,

---

[6] Contributors are Richard A. Lanham, Josephine Miles, J. Hillis Miller, Wayne C. Booth, David Bleich, Nancy R. Comley and Robert Scholes, Elaine P. Maimon, Walter J. Ong, S. J., E. D. Hirsch, Jr., David S. Kaufer and Richard E. Young, Frederick Crews, and Edward P. J. Corbett.

and scrutiny of my ideologies would enable one to predict my literary tastes. In any case, my argument in this book can be viewed as an expression of my admiration for the authors that I discuss and of the pleasure that I take in their writings.

CHAPTER 2

The Rhetoric of Presentation

Insofar as a choice of *action* is restricted, rhetoric seeks rather to have a formative effect upon *attitude* (as a criminal condemned to death might by priestly rhetoric be brought to an attitude of repentance and resignation). Thus, in Cicero and Augustine there is a shift between the words "move" (*movere*) and "bend" (*flectere*) to name the ultimate function of rhetoric. This shift corresponds to a distinction between act and attitude (attitude being an incipient act, a leaning or inclination). Thus the notion of persuasion to *attitude* would permit the application of rhetorical terms to purely *poetic* structures; the study of lyrical devices might be classed under the head of rhetoric, when these devices are considered for their power to induce or communicate states of mind to readers, even though the kinds of assent evoked have no overt, practical outcome.

—Kenneth Burke, *A Rhetoric of Motives* (50)

Recently my 28-month-old grandson and I lived a fiction. The family were having dinner out. Chris becoming squirmy, he and I repaired to a small rock garden in the front of the restaurant, where we stepped up on a large boulder, perhaps two feet high, better to contemplate the world of Western Avenue in Los Angeles. "Poppy," said Chris, "we're so high. How we gonna get down?"

"Maybe we can call a helicopter," I suggested.

"Nah," he said. "How about a beanstalk?"

"But that would take too long to grow."

"Poppy, I'll call Meemoo," and in a tragic voice, he shouted, "Meemoo, Meemoo, help! Help!"

His grandmother not responding, he said to me, "Poppy, let's cry," and we both wept pitifully for a couple of minutes.

Since Meemoo, Mommy, and Daddy now appeared, the game ended, and we all went home to begin yet another game, the details of which I will spare you.

It seems to me that explaining this game is hardly more complicated than the game itself. The "primary framework" for the game might, in Goffman's terminology, be called "danger in high places," the features of which were known to both Chris and me, though, certainly, we had never discussed the "genre." We then "keyed" this framework, that is, we pretended to follow the "rules" for "danger in high places" even though we were not in danger or in a high place.

If there were not situations of real danger in high places, the game would have had no meaning. If Chris and I had not entered the tacit contract to act *as if* we were in such a situation, there would have been no game.

Now it is possible to say that we were *interpreting* history or *asserting* something about it, in that every action is a response to a historical situation, but it seems to me that this formulation is cumbersome and, finally, untrue to the human situation. People *do* play—hearts, tag, tennis, poker. I have no doubt that there are deep psychological reasons for these games in the sense that there are deep psychological (and "scenic") reasons for all human *actions*, but why insist that fictions—even documentary fictions—are telic? Whether or not Richard Lanham is correct in attributing the play motive to an inherited "biogrammar," he assuredly has history on his side when, in *Literacy and the Survival of Humanism*, he says,

[R]hetoric accepted two areas of human motive which Platonic philosophy did not—game and play. Game meant the whole area of ludic struggle, of invidious comparison, of status-seeking, of everything that Christianity was to call pride. Play meant the spontaneous need to engage in certain attitudes whether they were elicited by pressing circumstance or not. Play was non-purposive motive, and since it lay outside the domain of rational (i.e., purposive) explanation, it was potentially subversive. (7)

This chapter will argue that presentational narrative is persuasive, but since it is also equipment for living, it is an agency of play. Using traditional principles of rhetoric as the scaffolding, we will deal with the problems of (1) assertion and argument from the standpoint of *logos;* (2) interpretation from the standpoint of *ethos;* and (3) persuasion from the standpoint of *pathos.*

The first chapter asked, "What *is* presentational literature?" The present chapter asks, "What does presentational literature *do?*"

The Speech Act

In order to keep the dialectic of this chapter intact, we must briefly cover some familiar territory, which Mary Louise Pratt, in *Toward a Speech Act Theory of Literary Discourse,* charted so well that I am tempted merely to quote her third chapter, "The Linguistics of Use"; however, the quick trip through the well-trodden paths of speech act theory will lead us to more exotic landscapes.

Speech act theory, as developed primarily by Austin and Searle, limited itself to the sentence, asking basically "What do sentences *do?*" In "A Classification of Illocutionary Acts," Searle answered that question as follows. As *representatives,* sentences make claims, hypothesize, describe, predict. . . . As *directives,* they request, plead, command. . . . As *commissives,* they promise, threaten, vow. . . . As *expressives,* they congratulate, thank, deplore, condole. . . . And as *declarations,* they baptize, pass sentence, christen. . . .

Speaking a sentence is performing three acts in one: "(a) Uttering words (morphemes, sentences) = performing *utterance acts.* (b) Referring and predicating = performing *propositional acts.* (c) Stating, questioning, commanding, promising, etc. = performing *illocutionary acts*" (*Speech Acts* 24). To these three acts, Searle adds J. L. Austin's *perlocutionary act,* the result of the speech act (*Speech Acts* 25). For example, a *claim* may convince the hearer, a *command* may bring about obedience, or a *threat* may arouse fear.

Now certain conditions must prevail for speech acts to be felicitous. Obviously, if I am not a judge acting within the scene of a court, my speech act "I hereby sentence you to thirty days in jail" does not count as a *declaration,* but probably would be interpreted as either some kind of indirect speech act or as mere nonsense. The details of Searle's logical analyses need not slow us down here. (For instance, on pages 57–61, he gives an analysis of *promising.*)

The Speech Act and Presentational Texts

As I mentioned in the previous chapter, Kenneth Burke has stated (during a 1977 conference at the University of Southern California) that the notion of attitude embraces the speech act theorists' *illocution;* attitude is antecedent, a necessary condition for the speech act.

What Burke saw that philosophers of language and linguists did not is that logically, each illocution must embody its corresponding perlocution. If a private says to a general, "I hereby order you to mop the barracks," the general will take the utterance as a true order *if he believes that the private believes that he (the private) has the authority to give such an order,* even though it may not be a lawful order sanctioned by the institution. On the other hand, the private can be sincere in his belief that he has the authority (e.g, from God, by his own code of ethics, from a misunderstanding of institutional laws) to issue a command to the general (whereas the general might take the private to be a wiseguy or a psychotic). From the standpoint of felicity conditions, a speech act may be a misfire and yet count as a straightforward speech act, not as fiction, a lie, or a figure of speech.

In "Epilogue: Prologue in Heaven," a masque from *The Rhetoric of Religion,*the Impresario tells us to "imagine such intuitive expression as a dialogue between two persons that are somehow fused with each other in a communicative bond whereby each question is its own answer, or is answered without being asked. Such is the formal paradox underlying the discourse between The Lord and Satan [in the masque]" (273).

Such also is the formal paradox underlying the lyric, which is a "pure" speech act, the utterance viewed only from the perspective of the speaker, who is simultaneously the hearer. The attitude danced in the lyric is both illocution (in the sense of intention) and perlocution (in the sense of uptake and result): "pure."

The Speech Act and the Traditional Principles of Rhetoric

In "Speech Acts and the Reader-Writer Transaction," Dorothy Augustine and I bridged the gap between speech act theory and rhetoric in the following way. To understand a sentence, you must attribute illocutionary force; that is, you must take the utterance as a statement, claim, promise, threat. . . . If you cannot determine what kind of illocution has been enacted, you do not understand the sentence even though you may understand all of the words in it. Thus, if Augustine and I say,

1.   The implications for rhetorical theory of research in philosophy and linguistics are rich.

and you take the utterance to be a statement, your understanding can be represented something like this:

2. [We hereby state to you that] The implications for rhetorical theory. . . .

We call the first proposition—*We hereby state to you (that)*—the rhetorical intention and the second proposition—*The implications for rhetorical theory of research,etc.*—the propositional intention. The rhetorical intention and the propositional intention taken together constitute the super-intention, thus:

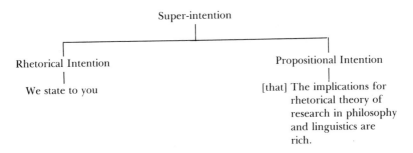

As we say, "Propositional intentions, then, account for most of the surface structure of what we read or hear in discourse. 'Rhetorical intentions,' indicative of and accounting for the *purpose* of introducing the proposition(s) of the subordinate clause are, for the most part, understood . . . much as is the deep-structure 'you' of the imperative" (131).

To get to the point of this extension of speech act theory, we can follow the *via negativa*, using two-sentence language games as handy case studies and asking not about speech acts that seem to work, but about some of those that go awry.

4. Speaker: [I hereby *claim* (to you that)] An asteroid will destroy the earth tomorrow at noon.
   Respondent: You don't know enough about astronomy to make such a claim.

5. S: [I hereby *inform* you (that)] You are a resident of California.
   R: But I already know that I'm a resident of California.

6. S: [I hereby *urge* you to] Vote a straight Republican ticket.
   R: Since I have voted Republican for the last twelve years, you must have me confused with my brother the Democrat.

The discourse in example 4 misfires because the respondent

doubts the credibility of the speaker, a problem of *ethos*. The discourse in example 5 misfires because the speaker does not actually inform the respondent of anything, a problem of *logos*. And the discourse in example 6 fails because the speaker has chosen the wrong addressee, a problem of *pathos*. These misfires, in other words, recapitulate the classical analysis of argument based on the character and credibility of the speaker (*ethos*), on the nature of the audience (*pathos*), and on the subject matter itself (*logos*).

However, if all felicity conditions have been met, hearers do not have the warrant to challenge the illocution conveyed by a verb such as *promise* or *admit*, for these verbs belong to a class that we might call *arhetorical*, which accounts for the following felicitous and infelicitous language games:

7.   S: [I admit to you that] I was mistaken.
     $H^{1:}$ Well, I'm glad you finally owned up to your error.
     $H^{2:}$ It is courageous of you to say so.
     $H^{3:}$ Welcome to the club!
     $H^{4:}$ In that case you're forgiven.
     $H^{5:}$ *You can't prove that.
     $H^{6:}$ *Are you certain of what you're saying?

Responses H^1-H^4 do not invite a counter-response; they are complete within the two sentences. Responses H^5 and H^6 are inappropriate since one does not argue about or question an admission (if the utterance counts as an admission). Argument begins when it is legitimate to negate or question the verb controlling the superintention—which is one reason why presentational texts, regardless of how persuasive they might be, are relatively impotent as arguments. But this is the topic of a later section of the present chapter. As we shall see, most texts are controlled by macropropositions which might be called superordinate speech acts. If these macropropositions cannot be challenged or negated, argument cannot ensue, and that is one of the primary differences between discursive and presentational texts.

Speech Acts and Macropropositions

The idea of the macroproposition is so commonplace as to need little discussion other than a few reminders of its various guises. Northrop Frye says that when we read a fictional work, continuity is the center of our attention; our later memory, or what I call the possession of it, tends to become discontinuous. Our attention shifts from the sequence of events to another focus: a sense of what the work of fiction was all *about*, or what criticism usually calls its theme. And we notice that as we go on to study and reread the work of fiction, we tend not to reconstruct the plot, but to become conscious of the theme, and to see all incidents as manifestations of it. ("Myth, Fiction, and Displacement" 23)

In *Macrostructures*, Teun A. van Dijk distinguishes *local* structures (e.g., syntax and cohesion relationships between sentences) and *global* structures (e.g., gist, thesis, theme). A coherent text is one that can be "treed" in a diagram extending downward from the macroproposition (187–89).

It is tempting to extend accepted speech act theory to the whole text, making the macroproposition a performative sentence like

8.   I hereby argue that in gaining culture mankind loses innocence.

which, of course, is Henry James' obsessive theme. But *The American, Portrait of a Lady, The Ambassadors,* and *The Golden Bowl* do not argue at all; they present or illustrate, and the following performative sentence, as applied to these novels, is infelicitous:

9.   *I hereby illustrate that in gaining culture humankind loses innocence.

If the speech act calculus of macropropositions is not as neat as that of sentences, nonetheless we can follow Pratt in salvaging an important principle from ordinary language philosophy—namely, the concept of "appropriateness conditions," by which term Searle indicates the "givens" necessary for a felicitous speech act. The three general categories of conditions are *preparatory, sincerity,* and *essential.* Thus, for an *assertion:*

Preparatory

1.   S[peaker] has evidence (reasons, etc.) for the truth of p[roposition].
2.   It is not obvious to both S and H[earer] that H knows (does not need to be reminded of, etc.) p.

Sincerity
S believes p.

Essential
> Counts as an undertaking to the effect that p represents an actual
> state of affairs (65).

Using the difference between telling a story and testifying in court
as an example, Pratt argues that appropriateness conditions apply
at the level of the discourse. "The court requires that the witness
not evaluate the events he recounts; the appropriateness conditions
on natural narrative require that he do so. In addition, the appropriateness conditions for natural narrative require that the speaker tell
a complete narrative (with complicating action and resolution) and
that he orient it adequately with respect to his audience" (85). Litera-
riness, fictionality, and poeticality are not functions of the text itself,
but result from the way in which the reader takes the text, using
the appropriateness conditions that constitute the genre. If, for
instance, the reader takes the nonfiction novel to be nonfiction, the
essential condition for assertions would apply: the work would be
taken as representing an actual state of affairs. Under this condition,
the obviously fictional elements in the text—such as invented dialogue—are taken as authorial interpretations, legitimate hypotheses
about reality, not as fictions, which is Barbara Foley's point when
she says that both fiction and nonfiction work within "totalizing
frames analogous to those explicitly formulated by psychology [the
figure can be either a rabbit or a duck, but not both simultaneously],
linguistics [specifically, the Chomskian notion of "competence"],
and the philosophy of science [according to which the explanatory
model—e.g, the Ptolemaic and Copernican views of the universe—
does not construct its data]" (40). Thus, the borders between fact
and fiction are sharply drawn through "a contract, wherein writer
and reader share an agreement about the conditions under which
texts can be composed and comprehended" (40).

It goes without saying, of course, that discursive texts often have
macropropositions that formally state a thesis and that, therefore,
invite dialectic.

The Cooperative Principle

Virtually everyone who writes about "the literature of fact" mentions a contract between the writer and the reader, a tacit agreement
about what the writer can and cannot do and the parameters of
reader response. In the expanded view of the literature of fact,

which includes both narrative and thematic texts, a reader-writer contract also prevails.

Though the theorists and critics who write about the literature of fact do not mention H. P. Grice, one suspects that their ideas of contract must derive ultimately from his "Cooperative Principle," which, in brief outline and applied to written discourse, goes something like this. The author tacitly promises (1) to give the readers all they need to know and nothing in excess (the maxim of *quantity*); (2) to be reliable and truthful (the maxim of *quality*); (3) not to introduce irrelevancies (the maxim of *relation*); and (4) to be as clear as possible (the maxim of *manner*). None of these principles is an absolute, each depending on the ratio among the writer's purpose, the readers, the scene, and the medium.

Writers, in all genres, violate the principles either unintentionally (through error or ineptitude) or intentionally (either to deceive or to achieve an effect such as humor or irony). The reader either tacitly ascribes an intention to the writer and interprets the cooperative situation according to that assumed intention or assumes that the violation is the result of error or ineptitude (which is the usual assumption regarding student papers; that is, Jonathan Swift, Charles Lamb, and George Orwell have the right to commit intentional violations of the cooperative principle, but students in freshman English do not).

It is worthwhile to examine how writers use the conventions of the cooperative principle to create their effects.

Joan Didion's characteristically laconic style is a good example of an author using the convention of *quantity* for her own purposes. Rather than the impleting characteristic of such authors as Mailer, Wolfe, Capote, and Lopez, Didion uses what Chris Anderson calls "radical particularity," which "in itself involves a kind of gap or silence" (137).

Rather than explain her feelings about the disjointedness of her own past [in "On Going Home"] Didion inventories childhood treasures: "A bathing suit I wore the summer I was seventeen. A letter of rejection from *The Nation,* an aerial photograph of the site for a shopping center my father did not build in 1954." Why didn't her father build the shopping center? And what does that fact mean? Why include it? Didion doesn't say. She lets the fact resonate. Rather than tell us that her family is uncommunicative and out of touch, she provides a one sentence dramatization: "We miss each other's points, have another drink, and regard the fire." Each scene is preceded or concluded with interpretive statements, but because these interpretive statements are short and suggestive rather than elaborated, the scenes bear most of the burden of significance. We must read them. (137–38)

The maxim of *quality* has to do with the reliability of the writer-narrator (and is related to ethical argument, to which we will turn in a moment). If we take the writer to be reliable, we accept even his or her obvious fictions as honest attempts at interpretation, which is why the conventions of invented dialogue or internal monologue in the nonfiction novel do not annihilate authorial credibility.

In *The Executioner's Song,* Norman Mailer plays with the convention of *quality* when he uses the following as an epigraph:

> Deep in my dungeon
>   I welcome you here
> Deep in my dungeon
>   I worship your fear
> Deep in my dungeon
>   I dwell.
> I do not know
>   if I wish you well.

Which he says is an *old prison rhyme*. In his afterword, as he is talking about the scrupulosity with which he attempted to adhere to facts, he makes this admission: "Finally, one would confess one's creations. The *old prison rhyme* at the beginning and end of this book is not, alas, an ancient ditty but a new one, and was written by this author ten years ago for his movie *Maidstone*" (1052).

On the one hand, Mailer in owning up to his fictionalizing, is coming clean and thus, at the very end of a very long "true life novel," is reestablishing his authority and credibility. On the other hand, he is admitting that he was willing to dupe the reader for more than a thousand pages.

In his use of the maxim of quality, Mailer is implying some extremely complex ideas concerning his book and placing on the reader the burden of separating imaginative creation from reporting and facts from *factoids*, a neologism that he defines as "facts which have no existence before appearing in a newspaper or magazine, creations which are not so much lies as a product to manipulate emotion in the Silent Majority" (*Marilyn* 18).

"Violation" of the maxim of *relation* often creates irony or humor. In *Rising from the Plains,* John McPhee's intricately woven account of geology and ranching in Wyoming, the author tells of the hard winter of 1912 and the spring flood in 1913 that virtually wiped out the Love family ranch. Deeply in debt, the Loves were forced to sell their sheep, their cattle, their horses, even their dogs.

As [John Love's] wife watched the finish of this scene, standing silent with Allan in her arms, the banker turned to her kindly and said, "What will you do with the baby?"
She said, "I think I'll keep him."

By intentionally misinterpreting the banker's intention and making a pseudo-irrelevant response, Mrs. Love shows both her own spirit and her attitude toward the commercial brutality of those who, in her opinion, had robbed the family of its hard-won assets. As for *manner,* the situation is fairly complex and involves *relative readability.* As we saw in the section on texture, propositions can be stated in sentences that vary in their difficulty for readers. Just as obviously, textured prose is more difficult to read than untextured (even though one's knowledge of the subject matter of the text is more salient than syntax in readability), but, as we will find hereafter, "reading involves a tradeoff between information and eloquence: the more we want information, the more we become annoyed by texture, and the less information we demand immediately, the more we enjoy eloquence for its own sake" (Winterowd, *Composition/Rhetoric* 65). In other words, *manner* is a matter of semantic intention, and no one would claim that a writer's style was intentionally more complex than warranted by semantic intention, for that is simply a logical contradiction.

Logos, Assertion, and Argument

Authors can tell the truth by writing fictions that use documentary techniques or by writing documentary accounts that use the techniques of fiction. We are concerned with the latter, but in regard to the former, Barbara Foley's *Telling the Truth: The Theory and Practice of Documentary Fiction* is essential, both in posing the right questions and in the distinctions that the author makes in her treatment of the issues involving what she calls "documentary fiction," the categories of which, she says, are (1) *the pseudofactual novel* of the

seventeenth and eighteenth centuries, which "simulates or imitates
the authentic testimony of a 'real life' person" (e.g., *Robinson Crusoe*);
(2) *the historical novel* of the nineteenth century (e.g., *War and Peace*);
and (3) *the documentary novel* of modernism, which consists of three
categories, (a) *the fictional autobiography* (e.g., *Portrait of the Artist*); (b)
the Afro-American documentary novel, which "represents a reality
submitting human subjects to racist objectification" (25; e.g., *Native
Son*); and (c) *the metahistorical novel,* which "takes as its referent a
historical process that evades rational formulation" (25), as in
Woolf's *Orlando,* "where documentary materials 'testify' not to the
validity of the text's interpretation of historical process but rather
to the necessity of forging an aesthetic that will transcend that
process altogether" (195–96).

With Gerald Graff, Edward Said, and others, Foley argues against
theories that claim the autonomy of literature: "Mimesis is, I propose, first and foremost *a mode of cognition,* enacted through a generic contract of which the purpose is to interpret and evaluate past
or present historical actuality" (64). As Graff says, the position that
poetry does not convey what he calls "propositional meaning"

tends to reduce poetry to a form of mythotherapy. The typical opposition
between propositional and presentational meaning renders the theorist's
well-intentioned appeals to the world of objective reality illegitimate and
induces him to obscure the distinction between what is true and what is
desirable. The separation of poetry and ideas tends to destroy the unity of
humanistic knowledge, intensifying the fragmentation which the theory
originally set out to repair. (24)

Assertion

As the first chapter indicated, the valuation of literature is a
paradox: the less *assertive* power a text is taken to possess, the more
worth it has as literature. As Foley says, in the theories of critics
who ignore the fact that mimesis entails a social contract, "Fiction's
impotence is . . . a peculiar correlative of its power" (42), and its
oxymoronic impotent power results from the failure to understand
that although a text invokes the "terms" of a mimetic "contract,"
"they do not in themselves constitute the essence of fictional discourse" (51), which is nothing less than the historical reality

as much present in *Slaughterhouse-Five* as it is in *Studs Lonigan,* insofar as
both texts aim to render the shape and essential development of historical

actuality, not primarily in its particulars, but in what the author sees as being its significant constitutive principles. The issue is not, then, that some fictional modes are more autotelic and others more referential; all are equally autotelic (configurational) and referential (analogous) at the same time. (72)

Vonnegut and Farrell do not assert that Billy Pilgrim and Studs ever existed, but the authors use every device at their command to convince readers that the "general propositions about life and destiny" are valid (72).

Argument

Foley's analysis of assertion in fictions yields precisely the dramatistic scene-agent lyric ratio: the works give us "historical actuality" (i.e., scene) from the standpoint of "what the author sees as being its significant constitutive principles," (i.e., from the standpoint of agent). Culturally, from classical times onward, the *rhetoric* of Western logic and dialectic has proscribed the foregrounding of agent, which is to say, that in logic the argument supposedly stands or falls according to its own structure and the evidence adduced, regardless of who is arguing; this rhetoric of logic consists in an elaborate set of conventions that are summarized by terms such as "objective," "disinterested," "logical," and "open-minded." I would stress that discourses recognized as arguments in the West result from *conventions,* not from a genetic endowment or from some Platonic model toward which all reasonable people strive. For example, in our own society, differing conventions of argument result in confrontation:

Present-day whites relate to their material as spokesmen, not advocates. This is because they believe that the truth or other merits of an idea are intrinsic to the idea itself. How deeply a person cares about or believes in the idea is considered irrelevant to its fundamental value. . . . Because blacks admit that they deal from a point of view, they are disinclined to believe whites who claim not to have a point of view, or who present their views in a manner that suggests that they do not themselves believe what they are saying. That is why they often accuse whites of being insincere. (Kochman 22–23)

Documentary fiction and its nonfiction counterpart *assert,* but they do not *argue* in the way that counts in our culture. The next question is "What do they *do?*" for the illocutionary act of asserting has its inevitable counterpart, the perlocution, the consequence of the illocution. This query shifts the discussion from poetic to rhetoric.

From the standpoint of rhetoric, both documentary fiction and presentational narrative have precisely the same status: neither serves well as an argument, though both genres can (1) support arguments and (2) serve as agencies of persuasion. Both *Slaughterhouse-Five* and *Studs Lonigan* may assert that the world is such-and-such, but neither argues the proposition *discursively,* a self-evident fact about these *presentational* texts.

Before too long, we will begin to discuss presentational literature as persuasion, but for the moment we will turn to Stephen Toulmin's analysis of argument to explain why presentational texts do not count for much in this genre. Toulmin says that the *claim* or argument proper, which might need *qualification,* is based on *evidence:*

> *Evidence:* This season Coach Honker has lost more games than he's won: five to one.
> *Claim:* Honker should resign.
> *Qualification:* unless he wins the rest of the games this season.

However, the arguer must supply a *link* between the evidence and the claim; the link may well need *backing* and often must be stated with a *reservation.*

> *Link:* The purpose of a coach is to win games,
> *Reservation:* unless the players are interested only
> in killing time and getting some exercise.
> *Backing:* We might remember the great coaches of
> history because of their qualities as
> human beings, but if they had not been
> winners, they wouldn't have had the chance
> to display that fine character.

Figure 2–1 is a diagram of this structure.

As an example of how argument does *not* work in presentational texts, I turn to *Dispatches,* by Michael Herr, a masterpiece, ranking, in my opinion, with *The Red Badge of Courage* and *The Naked and the Dead* as an account of war. Whether or not one agrees with my admiration for the book, it is clearly a work for which readers

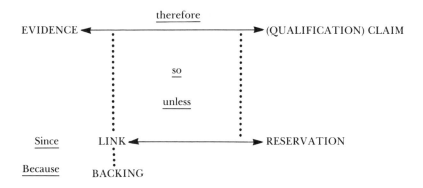

Figure 2-1. Stephen Toulmin's structure of argument. (The schematic was developed by Erwin P. Bettinghouse, in Charles W. Kneupper, "Teaching Argument: An Introduction to the Toulmin Model," *College Composition and Communication* 29 [Oct. 1978]: 238.)

have great esteem, and one that consciously repudiates "objective" reporting—the primary imagination's copy—in favor of imitation. (Rather than "copy" and "imitation," I could have chosen other terms from the "screen" that the first chapter developed.)

In Vietnam, "The press got all the facts (more or less), it got too many of them. But it never found a way to report meaningfully about death, which of course was really what it was all about" (229). After an interview with General Westmoreland, Herr "came away feeling as though I'd just had a conversation with a man who touches a chair and says, 'This is a chair,' points to a desk and says, 'This is a desk'" (231). Conventional discursive journalism "could no more reveal this war than conventional firepower could win it, all it could do was take the most profound event of the American decade and turn it into a communications pudding, taking its most obvious, undeniable history and making it into a secret history. And the very best correspondents knew even more than that" (232).

On one memorable afternoon, a special briefing, attended by many reporters, outlined the Pacification program, but Herr opted not to attend, spending the time in a bar talking to soldiers from the 1st Infantry Division, the famous Big Red One.

One of them was saying that the Americans treated the Vietnamese like animals.

"How's that?" someone asked.

"Well, you know what we do to animals . . . kill 'em and hurt 'em. Shit, we don't treat the Dinks no different than that."

And we knew that he was telling the truth. He wasn't judging it, I don't think that he was even particularly upset about it, it was just something he'd observed. You only had to look at his face to see that he really knew what he was talking about. We mentioned it later to some people who'd been at the Pacification briefing, someone from the *Times* and someone from the AP, and they both agreed that the kid from the Big Red One had said more about the Hearts-and-Minds program than they'd heard in over an hour of statistics, but their bureaus couldn't use this story, they wanted Ambassador Komer's. And they got it and you got it. (234)

This "representative anecdote" is, in a way, *Dispatches* in miniature, extremely *persuasive* (for me, at least), but not *convincing* because it does not "count" as evidence:

"What's your *evidence* for the *claim* that you can't get the real truth about Vietnam from official sources?"

"Well, while the ambassador was briefing the press, I was in a bar talking with this GI from The Big Red One. . . . "

or backing:

"You seem to be implying that official sources use 'facts' as a diversion, which is the *link* between your claim and your evidence. What is your *backing* for this link?"

"You only had to look at his face to see that he really knew what he was talking about."

Of course, I am not demeaning *Dispatches*, though to say that it is persuasive is to devalue it since literature should be impotent. (I have paused a considerable piece over the term "impotent," with all of its sexist connotations, and the fact that I do not replace it indicates that I choose to have it resonate in the present context.)

In his chapter on "The Multiplicity of Writing" from *Marxism and Literature*, Raymond Williams, in a most commonsense way, razes the distinction between "imaginative" texts that purportedly do not assert and "nonimaginative" that do, for the "range of actual writing . . . surpasses any reduction of 'creative imagination' to the 'subjective', with its dependent propositions: 'literature' as 'internal' or 'inner' truth; other forms of writing as 'external' truth" (148).

Ethos and Interpretation

In *The Mythopoeic Reality: The Postwar American Nonfiction Novel*, Mas'ud Zavarzadeh argued that the nonfiction novel is the response of people who find modern reality so puzzling, so bizarre, that interpretation is impossible. The facts themselves are, according to the irresistible cliché, "stranger than fiction." The tradition of the "liberal-humanist" novel with its "totalization" of experience lives on in the works of Bellow, Malamud, and Updike, but Pynchon, Barthelme, and Katz "have repudiated the claims of the totalizing novel to an integrated view of existing realities" (4).

Moving in the opposite direction, nonfiction novelists, through a neutral registration of experiential situations, have captured the fictive nature of technetronic culture. They reject the conventional notions of art as the creation of order out of chaos and the writer as seer. In their works the mythic underside of the surrealistic facts of post-industrial society is revealed and the indeterminacy of truth in extreme situations where fact and fiction converge is enacted. (4)

Thematic texts are by definition interpretations: that is the whole purpose of, for instance, the personal essay. However, narratives are equally interpretive, for making a story is creating an interpretation.

History as Story as Interpretation

Hayden White's central point in "The Fictions of Factual Representation" is that poets might be dealing with imaginary events, and historians with "factual" events, but the process of fusing them into a coherent whole is the same, a "poetic" process. A chronicle, a list of "raw" facts, becomes history when the historian fashions it as a story with *inaugural, terminating,* and *transitional motifs* (5), giving significant form to a swatch of history through language, "the *instrument of mediation* between consciousness and the world that consciousness inhabits" (29).

In "The Art of Fiction," Henry James had said virtually the same thing. The novel must "speak with the assurance, with the tone of the historian" (30). James found, much to his disappointment, that Trollope off and on again reminded the reader of the fiction, which James considered "a terrible crime" (30).

It implies that the novelist is less occupied in looking for the truth (the truth, of course I mean, that he assumes, the premises that we grant him, whatever they may be) than the historian, and in so doing it deprives him at a stroke of all his standing room. To represent and illustrate the past, the actions of men, is the task of either writer, and the only difference that I can see is, in proportion as he succeeds, to the honor of the novelist, consisting as it does in his having more difficulty in collecting his evidence, which is so far from being purely literary. (31)

If Roman Jakobson is correct, says White, great works of fiction will not be "about" only their subject matter, but about language itself "and the problematic relationship between language, consciousness, and reality" (32). And that will also be the case with the great historians.

Any given linguistic protocol will obscure as much as it reveals about the reality it seeks to capture in an order of words. This *aporia* or sense of contradiction residing at the heart of language itself is present in *all* of the classic historians. It is this linguistic self-consciousness which distinguishes them from their mundane counterparts and followers, who think that language can serve as a perfectly transparent medium of representation and who think that if one can only find the right language for describing events, the meaning of the events will *display itself* to consciousness. (36–37)

In this statement, White is recapitulating one of Kenneth Burke's central doctrines—regarding terminologies and representative anecdotes.

Literature as Equipment for Living

One of Burke's most apt titles is almost a thesis statement for the essay that it names: "Literature as Equipment for Living," an early (1941) counterstatement to the developing objectivist New Criticism. He begins with a discussion of proverbs, saying that in "more or less homey and picturesque ways" they "chart" situations (253). "Here is no 'realism for its own sake.' Here is realism for promise, admonition, solace, vengeance, foretelling, instruction, charting, all for the direct bearing that such acts have upon matters of welfare" (255). Well, then, why not apply the same kind of analysis to all of literature? Doing so, literary works become strategies for dealing with situations, and "Another name for strategies might be *attitudes*" (256).

Of course, strategies can be oversimplified, unrealistic, or merely self-gratifying. "So the wise strategist . . . will 'keep his weather eye open'" (257) and will not fall for such alluringly simplified strategies as those provided by popular inspirational literature. "We usually take it for granted that people who consume our current output of books on 'How to Buy Friends and Bamboozle Oneself and Other People' are reading as *students* who will attempt applying the recipes given. Nothing of the sort. *The reading of a book on the attaining of success is in itself the symbolic attainment of that success.* It is *while they read* that these readers are 'succeeding'" (258).

In *A Grammar of Motives*, Burke initiates his dialectic regarding the uses of what he calls "representative anecdotes" which serve as the basis for a terminology (or calculus) to deal with situations.

For instance, the behaviorist uses his experiments with the conditioned reflex as the anecdote about which to form his vocabulary for the discussion of human motives; but this anecdote, though notably *informative*, is not *representative*, since one cannot find a representative case of human motivation in animals, if only because animals lack that property of linguistic rationalization which is so typical of human motives. A representative case of human motivation must have a strongly linguistic bias, whereas animal experimentation necessarily neglects this. (59)

The person who uses chemical experiments as his or her representative anecdote and says that humans are nothing but chemicals talks to people to bring about responses, but would not use the same tactic on chemicals (59).

The representative anecdote with enough scope contains *in nuce* a terminology adequate to deal with the situation of which the anecdote is representative. If, for example, we undertook an inquiry about the nature of dialectic, we might choose a railway terminal. "The name, 'Grand Central,' may have secretly moved us to hit upon the expression 'grand converge.' And in meditating upon a *terminal* we were certainly quite close to the problem of *terms*" (326). Yet this physicalist reduction, in spite of obvious advantages, lacked the necessary scope to accommodate "an interwovenness of traditions, needs, and expectancies" that Burke vaguely glimpsed. Ultimately he chose constitutions as suitable for his purposes (323–401).

Since the representative anecdote serves as a basis for deriving a terminology to deal with historical situations, it need not purport to be "realistic" or factual. (In what sense is a railway terminal a realistic or factual representation of dialectic?) From a presentational text (as from one that is discursive), I can derive my terminology, my strategies for encompassing situations, and it is just this sense in which literature is equipment for living.

We have seen that an appropriate representative anecdote yields a terminology for analyzing a situation. Now a terminology is both a *reflection* and a *selection* of reality, in other words, an interpretation. "Insofar as the vocabulary meets the needs of reflection, we can say that it has the necessary scope. In its selectivity, it is a reduction. Its scope and reduction become a deflection when the given terminology, or calculus, is not suited to the subject matter which it is designed to calculate" (*Grammar* 59).

For providing terminologies, history and fiction are equally useful. The less a factual narrative is a chronicle, the more it is like a novel, for it is the storyteller's craft that creates history.

A chronicle (perhaps) does not interpret, nor (ostensibly) does a news report in the *New York Times*, but once the chronicle or the newspaper article becomes the basis for history, documentary fiction, the nonfiction novel, or the novel, interpretation comes about. To borrow a metaphor from Henry James, "The story and the novel, the idea and the form, are the needle and thread, and I never heard of a guild of tailors who recommended the use of the thread without the needle, or the needle without the thread" ("The Art of Fiction" 40). The novel, in fact, is the treatment, the interpretation of the story. In chapter 5, "Form: The Essay," we will see how Loren Eiseley uses representative anecdotes heuristically.

The representative anecdote is clearly different from what might be called the "explanatory anecdote," that is, a story that either illustrates or clarifies a point in some way.

In "Ernest Freedberg's World," from the collection *Adventures of a Bystander*, Peter F. Drucker comments,

There are lots of people with grasshopper minds who can only go from one specific to another—from stockings to buttons, for instance, or from one experiment to another—and never get to the generalization and the concept. They are to be found among scientists as often as among merchants. But I have learned that the mind of the good merchant, as also of the good artist or good scientist, works the way Uncle Henry's mind worked. It starts out with the most specific, the most concrete, and then reaches for the generalization. (201–202)

Drucker then recounts a story about Charles Kellstadt, retired head of Sears Roebuck and consultant to the Department of Defense during the Kennedy administration. One day, a McNamara "whiz kid," an assistant secretary, presented a new way of defense pricing, but an unimpressed Kellstadt began to tell a story about the bargain basement of a store in Chillicothe, Ohio, where he had been manager. The tale involved a problem with the size of women's bras.

He would stop every few sentences and ask the bewildered Assistant Secretary a question about bras, then go on. Finally the Assistant Secretary said, "You don't understand, Mr. Kellstadt; I'm talking about concepts." "So am I," said Charlie, quite indignant, and went on. Ten minutes later all of us on the board realized that he had demolished the entire proposal by showing us that it was far too complex, made far too many assumptions, and contained far too many ifs, buts, and whens. . . . When we went out of the meeting, another board member, the dean of a major engineering school, said admiringly, "Charlie, that was a virtuoso performance. But why did you have to drag in the cup sizes of the bras in your bargain basement forty years ago?" Charlie was quite surprised. "How else can I see a problem in my mind's eye?" (202–3)

This anecdote is a "clincher," not a heuristic. It gives Drucker's abstract concept *presence* (which is in the following section).

Pathos and Persuasion

In a formal argument concerning the Vietnam War, *Dispatches*, as we have seen, would not hold up well except as an example of one observer's impressions and opinions, but we are certain that it is an extremely persuasive document. Presentational literature in general is persuasive—has "a formative effect on attitude." Three reasons for this potency are the *presence* that characterizes presentational texts, the *form* that predominates in them, and their ability to create *identification*.

Presence

Presence, that property that gives arguments status, vividness, and "extralogical" power, seems to have three aspects. First, the act of attention confers presence; that is, whatever we pay attention to in a text gains presence. Second, images create presence. Third, presence is conferred by holism (Winterowd, *Composition/Rhetoric* 152). In *The New Rhetoric*, Chaim Perelman and L. Olbrechts-Tyteca say that

> *Presence* acts directly on our sensibility. As Piaget shows, it is a psychological datum operative already at the level of perception: when two things are set side by side, say a fixed standard and things of variable dimensions with which it is compared, the things on which the eye dwells, that which is best or most often seen, is, by that very circumstance, overestimated. . . . Certain masters of rhetoric, with a liking for quick results, advocate the use of concrete objects in order to move an audience. . . . It should also be observed that the effort to make something present to the consciousness can relate not only to real objects, but also to a judgment or an entire argumentative development. As far as possible, such an effort is directed to filling the whole field of consciousness with this presence so as to isolate it, as it were, from the hearer's overall mentality. (116–18)

The classic example of presence is the emperor who noticed an ox being led before the palace and asking why was told that the animal was being taken to sacrificial slaughter. "Choose another animal for sacrifice," said the emperor, "one that I have not seen."

Actually, no one has said it better than Francis Bacon: "The affection beholdeth merely the present: reason beholdeth the future and sum of time. And therefore the present filling the imagination more, reason is commonly vanquished; but after that force of eloquence and persuasion hath made things future and remote appear as present, then upon the revolt of the imagination reason prevaileth."

I am not belittling Richard Marius's magnificent biography of Thomas More when I say that it has less potential for presence (*not* less potential for interest) than Jay Martin's equally magnificent biography of Henry Miller: the difference between the two is one of semantic intention (and, of course, availability of sources). Marius, it seems, adheres to a scrupulous standard of objectivity while Martin's purpose is to give an *honest* subjective reaction. Two characteristic passages from the works make the point better than pages of commentary. Here is the drama of Thomas More, grappling with the problem of "Priesthood or Marriage?"

> In 1519, when Erasmus described More's abstemious nature, he probably—without quite knowing it himself—gave us a man whose views on sensual pleasure were much like St. Augustine's; it was not that the plea-

sures of the senses were harmful merely when they were taken in excess; they were a sign of wickedness merely by their being, and the Christian should limit indulgence in them as much as possible. The worst of sensual sins, according to Augustine, was sexuality. As a Christian who believed in the doctrine of creation, he had to believe that marriage and childbearing accomplished a divine purpose since society required a steady supply of new life to take the place of the old that died. But since sexual intercourse was almost impossible to isolate from intense sensual pleasure, he could not view sexuality without a certain loathing, and at times he came very close to saying that sexual intercourse is a sign of depravity. He had had a mistress when he was young. When he became a Christian, he put her away, although he had had a son by her, Adeodatus, whose name means "Gift of God." His primary view of Christian salvation was that it was redemption from sensuality, which, if indulged in unchecked, would lead the soul directly to hell. He never ceased to exhort Christians to chastity, by which he meant abstention from sexual intercourse, and even when he praised marriage, he took care to say that virginity or abstinence was a higher state. Always, in his view, the man who succumbed to the sensuality of marriage was inferior to the person to whom God gave the gift of surmounting passion. (Marius 36–37)

With Richard Marius, we are in the realm of first-rate discursive narrative. With Martin, we move to presentation:

He was swimming in a sea of sperm, in a storm that was raging almost out of control. Pauline was a delicate but fully passionate woman who knew how to please a man, and herself. Every time she and Henry got near her house, the drums of love started throbbing, increasing as he followed her up the stairs. She would giggle with pleasure and anticipation as he ran his hand up her dress. The pulsations receded for a moment as she made sure that George, dying in the next room, was thoroughly tucked in. They undressed in the steaming kitchen. Carefully, deliberately, Pauline hung her clothes on a nail in the door, in an unintended striptease. First she slid out of her dress. Then came the corset and stays. Her breasts swung heavily as she bent over to step out of her stiffly starched pantaloons. Finally she removed her stockings: often these had different colored tops sewn to them from discarded hose. It excited Henry to see the colored silk pulled tight against her transparently white skin just below her big bush, its hairs already so moist they were plastered on her belly and legs. This was the burlesque of his dreams. He'd become so absorbed in watching, he'd almost forgot to undress himself. But the fucking began almost immediately—in the tubs, on the tables and floor, with her straddling him on a kitchen chair, or him picking her up and walking around the room carrying her while she squirmed around on him. It was an explosion. (25–26)

The rhetorical difference between these two passages depends on such minutiae as a nail in a door. "Carefully, deliberately, Pauline hung her clothes on a nail in the door, in an unintended striptease." It matters not one whit whether Martin has documentary evidence that the nail—and the ritual for which it stands—existed in historical fact. The nail in the door is interpretive and rhetorical. It is a significant aspect of presence, and it would be, as Plato put it in the *Phaedrus,* boorish wisdom to argue whether or not there was an actual nail. The truth of the account transcends its factuality.

Form

One of Kenneth Burke's most useful insights is that concerning "the psychology of information" and "the psychology of form," which is to say that the more we are interested in information, the less we are interested in form, defined by Kenneth Burke as "an arousing and fulfillment of desires. A work has form in so far as one part of it leads a reader to anticipate another part, to be gratified by the sequence" (*Counter-Statement* 124). The tradeoff between the informational and the formal is this: "The hypertrophy of the psychology of information is accompanied by the corresponding atrophy of the psychology of form" (*Counter-Statement* 33). The more we view either Hunter Thompson's *Hell's Angels* or Annie Dillard's *Pilgrim at Tinker Creek* as sources of information, the less we view them as esthetic objects. (I can view anything as an esthetic object, even the instructions for using a pay phone. When I do so, I am attending—largely, at least—to other than what information I can gain from the object: esthetic and informational reading involve different attitudes or motives.)

Burke makes a crucial distinction regarding form in texts:

Syllogistic progression is the form of the perfectly conducted argument, advancing step by step. . . . *Qualitative progression,* the other aspect of progressive form, is subtler. Instead of one incident in the plot preparing us for some other possible incident of plot . . . the presence of one quality prepares us for the introduction of another. . . . In T. S. Eliot's *The Waste Land,* the step from "Ta ta. Goonight. Goonight" to "Good night, ladies, good night, sweet ladies" is qualitative progression. (*Counter-Statement* 124–25).

It would perhaps not be heresy to apply new terms, substituting *logical* for syllogistic and *lyrical* for qualitative, the presence of one *attitude* preparing us for the introduction of another. If this arithmetic is correct, then we can say that the lyrical aspect of form is an element of persuasion in the presentational text. Lyrical progression leads to conclusions just as surely as does logical, but to state that we read for the lyric experience is to be utterly truistic.

The structure of such "nature meditations" (a genre that will be discussed hereafter) as *The Snow Leopard,* by Peter Matthiessen, *Desert Solitaire,* by Edward Abbey, and *Arctic Dreams,* by Barry Lopez, is qualitative progression, of which the brief concluding chapter of *Desert Solitaire* is a perfect example.

It begins abruptly: "The tourists have gone home. Most of them." And now it's time for the author, Edward Abbey, to leave the Arches National Monument, where he has spent the summer as a ranger, and return to New York. "Who am I to pity the degradation and misery of my fellow citizens? I, too, must leave the canyon country, if only for a season, and rejoin for the winter that miscegenated mesalliance of human and rodent called the rat race (*Rattus urbanus*). Today is my last day at the Arches; tonight I take a plane for Denver and from there a jet flight to New York" (297–98).

Everything is packed. The old pickup is winterized and on blocks in a friend's backyard. And Abbey is ready to depart.

That somewhat bitter, though matter-of-fact, exposition out of the way, the author turns again to the subject of the book: the natural world.

October. Rabbitbrush in full bloom. The tumbleweeds on the move (that longing to be elsewhere, elsewhere), thousands of them rolling across the plains before the wind. Something like yellow rash has broken out on the mountainsides—the aspen forests in their autumn splendor. Sunsets each evening that test a man's credulity—great gory improvisations in scarlet and gold that remind me of nothing so much as God's own celestial pizza pies. Followed inevitably by the night with its razzle-dazzle of stars in silver, emerald and sapphire blue, the same old routine. (299–300)

The modulation in this paragraph, from unspoiled nature to images of pizza pie and razzle-dazzle stars (like sequins?) is the progression of the author's attitude as he prepares for six months as a social worker in the city. And nature itself is not so perfect: the aspens are a golden "rash"; the sunsets are "gory improvisations."

Still, as Abbey is driven to the train station in Thompson, Utah, he says,

"Ferris, stop this car. Let's go back."
But he only steps harder on the gas. "No," he says, "you've got a train to catch." He sees me craning my neck to stare backward. "Don't worry," he adds, "it'll all still be here next spring."
The sun goes down, I face the road again, we light up our after-dinner cigars. Keeping the flame alive. The car races forward through a world dissolving into snow and night.
Yes, I agree, that's a good thought and it better be so. Or by God there might be trouble. The desert will still be here in the spring. And then comes another thought. When I return will it be the same? Will I be the same? Will anything ever be quite the same again? If I return. (303)

This, it seems to me, is an enormously powerful conclusion to an exceptionally fine book. The reader is led attitudinally to the final questions, which are in themselves, discursively, so trite as to be a liability. Strip the final chapter of *Desert Solitaire* of its qualitative, lyric progression, and only pabulum remains.

Strip presentational literature of its rhetorical force, and only pabulum remains.

CHAPTER 3
Ethos and *Pathos:*
Presentational Narrative

You persuade a man only insofar as you can talk his language by speech,
gesture, tonality, order, image, attitude, idea, *identifying* your ways with his.
— Kenneth Burke, *A Rhetoric of Motives* (55)

In this chapter, I would like to discuss the ethical and pathetic
appeal of a spectrum of works, ranging (in my calculus) from the
discursive (e.g., *Hiroshima*) through *Friendly Fire* to *Dispatches, Let Us
Now Praise Famous Men,* and *Armies of the Night* at the presentational
end of the spectrum. I will not carry out close *explication de texte,*
but will use the books as cases in point regarding my thesis about
literature. I will use *In Cold Blood* and *The Executioner's Song* contrapuntally, for the "news" that I have concerning them will develop
indirectly, through discussions of the other works.

I will start with some comments on the reader-writer "contract"
that seems to prevail with the sorts of texts that I am dealing with
and then will go on to discuss a group of narratives, beginning, for
reasons that will become obvious, with Irving Stone's *Passions of the
Mind.*

The Writer-Reader Contract

Any kind of language transaction operates according to a set of
tacit rules or rules-of-thumb, of which the cooperative principle is
the handiest example. However, the reader's and writer's shared
knowledge of genre also creates a contract whereby the nonfiction
novel and other "literature of fact" narratives are made possible.
In *Telling the Truth,* Barbara Foley is right on target when she

51

says, "Mimesis is, I propose, first and foremost *a mode of cognition, enacted through a generic contract*" (64). John Hellmann, though he does not cite Grice, comes up with what is almost a formalized cooperative principle. The realistic novelist says, "*All this did not really happen, but it could have*" (11). The fabulist says, "*All of this could never happen, so do not blame me if it does not seem real*" (11). The new journalist says, "*All this actually did happen, so do not blame me if it does not seem real*" (11).

The contract is invoked by a number of textual features, the most obvious and simple being a subtitle, as in *History as a Novel, The Novel as History*, the subtitle of *The Armies of the Night*. Texture, as discussed above, can be a tip-off, as can novelistic techniques.

Frye's distinction of inward and outward reference differentiates fiction from factual narrative, the fiction demanding that the reader not refer outside the text (for example, to an encyclopedia, *Current Biography*, or *Who's Who*) for knowledge of the characters and scenes, as if the author were saying, "You can't know anything about this character or these actions and scenes because they don't exist in reality; therefore, direct your attention to my narrative, and you will learn. The point of my story is to invent the characters, scenes, and actions." This is why in Hellmann's view the new journalism (or literature of fact) is "most properly understood as a genre of literature. Like realistic fiction or romantic fiction or fabulist fiction, it has an aesthetic form and purpose making its 'final direction' inward" (24). We can see this "endophoric" direction even at the very beginnings of nonfiction narratives, as in the first paragraph of *The Executioner's Song*: "Brenda was six when she fell out of the apple tree. She climbed to the top and the limb with the good apples broke off. Gary caught her as the branch came scraping down. They were scared. The apple trees were their grandmother's best crop and it was forbidden to climb in the orchard. She helped him drag away the tree limb and they hoped no one would notice. That was Brenda's earliest recollection of Gary" (5).

Who is Brenda? What is her significance? In fact, by the conventions of beginnings in fiction, the reader knows that answers to these questions are to be found within the text, not outside it—even though, in fact, Brenda Brown and Gary Gilmore were historical personages.

When we take authorial intention to have been literary, not merely communicative or informative, we gain the right to criticize, for the term "literature" is normative, very much like the term "joke." We judge jokes to be "funny," "dumb," "vulgar," "corny," "subtle," and so on; we judge joke tellers to be masterful or inept. And we render the same sorts of judgments on literary texts and their authors. Though certainly, as Pratt argues, giving up the right to respond in a dialogue creates the right to criticize a monologue (100–116), a condition that prevails in both literary and nonliterary discourse, the difference between a book review and a letter arguing against the position stated in a newspaper editorial is enough evidence that critical canons for texts that are *taken to be* literary are different from those that are taken to be nonliterary.

Foley's argument that both fiction and nonfiction work within totalizing frames is, it seems to me, one of the essentials regarding the experience of reading not only documentary fiction, but also such nonfiction works as *In Cold Blood,* which we take to be a "true" account of a historical event, even though it is perfectly obvious that much of the substance of the book is invented by the *imaginative* author, not merely set forth by the reliable reporter.

One hardly needs a mountain of evidence to validate the statement that readers take a work to be either fact or fiction even though the fiction may contain many elements of fact and the factual account may have fictional elements. (Foley deals usefully with this point on pages 25–41.) It is worth reminding ourselves that the great realistic novel of the nineteenth century was based on the factuality of its setting.

It being axiomatic that we read a text either as a factual account or as a fiction, but not as both simultaneously, we must explain the obviously fictional (nonfactual) elements of, for instance, the nonfiction novel, in which extensive dialogue, after the manner of fiction, is an element. Without the dialogue, the characters would not come to life, and the result would be, perhaps, documentary narrative, but not a nonfiction novel.

Why Irving Stone Is Popular

Irving Stone has been one of the most popular writers in America, having produced ten "biographical novels" (on, e.g., Van Gogh, Eugene V. Debs, Michelangelo, and Freud), four biographies (Jack London, Clarence Darrow, Earl Warren, and "defeated presidential candidates"), and various other original works and edited collections. His technique is to pack his work with factual information regarding scene and then fictionalize some acts, such as conversations. For example, sections of *Passions of the Mind* read almost as if they had come from the Baedeker guide to Vienna:

> From their apartment the Breuers could see the noble spire at the rear of St. Stephan's Cathedral, the two Romanesque towers at the front, the sharply slanting mosaic slate roof, the giant bell, *Pummerin*, the Boomer, which summoned the city to fires as well as worship. First started in 1144, when it stood outside the original medieval walls, the cathedral was, like the capital it served, a fascinating potpourri of seven centuries of architecture. (34)

The problem with the facts is that they have no motivation within the fiction; they rely entirely on what Kenneth Burke calls "the psychology of information" for their appeal, as does Baedeker.

In *Counter-Statement*, Kenneth Burke puts it this way: "Truth in art is not the discovery of facts, not an addition to human knowledge in the scientific sense of the word. It is, rather, the exercise of human propriety, the formulation of symbols which rigidify our sense of poise and rhythm. Artistic truth is the externalization of taste" (42).

Stone provides his readers with laypersons' introductions to art (*Lust for Life*), archaeology (*The Greek Treasure*), and, in *The Passions of the Mind*, psychoanalysis:

> He [Freud] had brought back from the summer vacation a piece of intellectual equipment which had not been part of his baggage when he left. While his feet had been treading the soft woodland paths of Untersberg, or the hand-made tiles of Venice's churches; while his eyes had been resting on the hundreds of variations of green in the dense forest, or the luscious colors of the Italian painters, a back area of his mind was becoming increasingly uneasy about the blame laid by his women patients on perverse acts by their fathers, evidence that had always astonished him, and which he had accepted reluctantly. He asked himself why, in those cases, he had failed to bring his analysis to a good conclusion. Why had some of his most responsive patients fled at a certain point, though some of their symptoms had abated? His findings had resoundingly demonstrated that the unconscious mind had no "indication of reality" and was unable to distinguish truth from emotionally charged fiction. (487)

Stone then takes us in some detail through the case study whereby Freud achieved his breakthrough and then to this commentary:

He had been right about infantile sexuality; it was there beyond question, earlier than anyone in the world had ever suspected or been willing to admit; but not as he had projected it. . . . It was with a profound sense of relief that he understood at last that ninety-nine percent of the relationships had never taken place; and yet his patients thought they had, and made themselves ill just as surely as though the sexual intimacy had occurred. (489)

One suspects that Stone's facts are accurate and that his outline of psychoanalytic theory is not wildly off the mark. Thus, in reading *The Passions of the Mind*, one is not merely idling time away, but is learning something, gaining the pleasure of story along with the uplift of knowledge. In fact, Stone is at his best *outside* the attitudinal and in the informational, for when one begins to look at qualitative progression and texture, one finds inappropriateness and patchwork, of which the following brief passage will be my only example: "The week before dragged. He tried to 'kill time,' which died reluctantly. The minutes were wet sponges underfoot; the more he tried to crush them out of existence the more they oozed on either side of his feet" (164). Block that metaphor!

The foremost problem with Stone's works is that he does not achieve qualitative coherence, his works veering from documentary factuality to fiction and back again. It is difficult for readers to maintain a consistent stance page after page when at one moment the author mines the ore of raw information (as in a guidebook or almanac), but then abruptly veers off into a dramatic seam.

Both *In Cold Blood* and *The Executioner's Song* are highly informative, but in a way quite different from that of *Passions of the Mind*, where one finds information apparently for its own sake.

Throughout *In Cold Blood*, Capote, like all good storytellers, has set the scene vividly. For example, after slaying the Clutter family Perry Smith and Richard Hickock took a crazy, dog-legged trip around the United States and Mexico, spending Christmas in Miami.

In Miami Beach, 335 Ocean Drive is the address of the Somerset Hotel, a small, square building painted more or less white, with many lavender touches, among them a lavender sign that reads, "*Vacancy—Lowest Rates— Always a Seabreeze.*" It is one of a row of little stucco-and-cement hotels lining a white, melancholy street. In December, 1959, the Somerset's "beach facilities" consisted of two beach umbrellas stuck in a strip of sand at the rear of the hotel. One umbrella, pink, had written on it, "We Serve Valentine Ice Cream." (199)

This information is integral to the qualitative progression of the story, carrying on the tone of melancholy shoddiness that is such an important aspect of the book's power.

Even when Capote provides information of the almanac sort, it is integral to the book's effect and apparent intention, not simply tacked on as an interesting by-the-way.

Convicted and sentenced to death, Perry and Dick are transported to the Kansas State Prison, about which we learn the following:

> Prisons are important to the economy of Leavenworth County, Kansas. The two state penitentiaries, one for each sex, are situated there; so is Leavenworth, the largest federal prison, and, at Forth Leavenworth, the country's principal military prison, the grim United States Army and Air Force Disciplinary Barracks. If all the inmates of these institutions were let free, they could populate a small city.
>
> The oldest of the prisons is the Kansas State Penitentiary for Men, a turreted black-and-white palace that visually distinguishes an otherwise ordinary rural town, Lansing. Built during the Civil War, it received its first resident in 1864. Nowadays the convict population averages around two thousand; the present warden, Sherman H. Crouse, keeps a chart which lists the daily total according to race (for example, White 1405, Colored 360, Mexicans 12, Indians 6). Whatever his race, each convict is a citizen of a stony village that exists within the prison's steep, machine-gun guarded walls—twelve gray acres of cement streets and cell blocks and workshops. (309)

The focus on scene becomes progressively sharper and more narrow, from Leavenworth County, to the Kansas State Prison for Men, and then to the dark, two-storied, coffin-shaped segregation and isolation building, and finally to "the twelve side-by-side cells that comprise Lansing's Death Row" (309).

The facts about Leavenworth County and its prisons are no less interesting than Stone's facts about Vienna, but Capote's factuality, like that of Dickens or Hardy, functions symbolically as well as informatively.

Gay Talese, whose works are quite properly esteemed as journalism, does not achieve the presentational intensity of *In Cold Blood* or *The Executioner's Song,* but he creates literature that is more satisfactory, in my view, than the montages of Stone's factual fictions. Talese's aim is to create literature that "can be as socially significant and as historically useful as the fictional lives and situations created by playwrights and novelists" (*Honor Thy Father* 17). "By writing about real people whose lives are touched by the issues of our time, and by using the narrative techniques of fiction in telling their stories, I have attempted to make comprehensible the complexity, and sometimes the hypocrisy, of the society in which we live" (18).

The purpose of a book such as *Honor Thy Father* is avowedly discursive, and I at least am quite willing to accept it on those terms so that the statistics and sermons with which the book is laced do contribute to the author's apparent intention.

By way of briefly comparing Talese with Stone, here are two characteristic passages from *Honor Thy Father,* the first a battery of statistics and the second a moral commentary:

In New York City alone in 1965, more than 400 arrests were made in organized crime. . . . Fourteen bolita operators were arrested in Tampa, Florida, by the Internal Revenue Service; 34 pimps, prostitutes, and gamblers were arrested in Columbus, Ohio, by the local police; 68 persons were arrested for illegal gambling in Chester, West Virginia, by the state police (156).

The numbers game is the national pastime of city slums, is a source of hope, however small, for the urban poor crowded into blocks of 10,000 people, living in teeming tenements each with its "runner," each with its corner store that may be a "drop" for numbered slips that are later picked up by "collectors" and delivered to "controllers" who record the data and later pay the winners. (157–58)

Like Mailer and Capote, Talese keeps his promises to the reader. For many readers (including me), the problem with *The Passions of the Mind* is that two contradictory reader-writer contracts are at work in it.

Ethical Appeal and the Unsayable in Narrative

Three superb books deal with the human consequences of war: *Hiroshima,* by John Hersey; *Friendly Fire,* by C. D. B. Bryan; and *Dispatches,* by Michael Herr—works that constitute a progression away from the objectively discursive and toward the presentational.

When *Hiroshima* appeared in 1946, reviews talked about what *Kirkus* called "the heights of impartial reporting" and generally praised the book for its "factual account, in straightforward reportorial style, of what happened in Hiroshima on the morning of August 6, 1945" (R. S. Hutchison, *Christian Century*, Sept. 25, 1946). The London *Times Literary Supplement* for December 7, however, said, "Mr. Hersey's style is flat, deliberately, no doubt, but it remains flat. There are one or two touches that must awe the most careless reader, such as the account of the soldiers whose eyes have melted away. But in general the effect is too quiet. Mr. Hersey has scrupulously let the facts speak for themselves, and they have not spoken loudly enough." What *TLS* apparently did not appreciate was Hersey's problem as an author: to convey a sense of what the Hiroshima bomb had done to a city and its people and to do this in such a way that the narrative would be humanly interesting, yet objective; factual, but not coldly clinical. To accomplish his purpose, Hersey told the story of six survivors: Miss Toshiko Sasaki, a clerk in the personnel department of the East Asian Tin Works; Dr. Masakazu Fujii, the proprietor of a one-doctor hospital; Mrs. Hatsuyo Nakamura, a widow; Father Wilhelm Kleinsorge, a German priest; Dr. Terufumi Sasaki, a young surgeon; and Reverend Mr. Kiyoshi Tanimoto, pastor of the Hiroshima Methodist Church. In telling the story of these survivors, Hersey created a book that moved from objective reporting toward the nonfiction novel, from discursiveness to presentation, but that, as we shall see, stopped well short of becoming fully presentational.

In *The Art of Readable Writing,* a book that aroused much comment (both favorable and unfavorable) when it was published in 1949, Rudolf Flesch says, "Only stories are readable" (72), and he quotes a *Reader's Digest* editor: "Whenever we want to draw attention to a problem, we wait until somebody does something about it. Then we print the story of how he did it" (p. 72). In effect, Flesch was stating the *scenario principle* of Linda Flower and John Hayes: functional prose should be structured around a human agent performing actions in an understandable context.

Hiroshima, a narrative, then, has an expository purpose. What one learns from the book is not data, but the experience of atomic devastation from the standpoint of six representative human beings, very much in the nature of case studies, more spare and synecdochic than the characters in *Friendly Fire* and *Dispatches.*

Hersey's narrative, in the first place, lacks the texturing that comes about through such novelistic devices as scenes that are detailed and become symbolic in the ways scenes in drama are appropriate settings for the actions; nor does one find the fullness of dialogue and status details mentioned by Hollowell (27–28). In the following typical passage, the scene of the action is a virtual schematic, and there is no dialogue, the third-person author reporting the thoughts of the characters and what they said. The bomb has just fallen, and Mr. Tanimoto, after recovering from his shock, runs to a mound in a neighbor's yard to look out over the city.

From the mound, Mr. Tanimoto saw an astonishing panorama. Not just a patch of Koi, as he had expected, but as much of Hiroshima as he could see through the clouded air was giving off a thick, dreadful miasma. Clumps of smoke, near and far, had begun to push up through the general dust. He wondered how such extensive damage could have been dealt out of a silent sky; even a few planes, far up, would have been audible. Houses nearby were burning, and when huge drops of water the size of marbles began to fall, he half thought that they must be coming from the hoses of firemen fighting the blazes. (They were actually drops of condensed moisture falling from the turbulent tower of dust, heat, and fission fragments that had already risen miles into the sky above Hiroshima.) Mr. Tanimoto turned away from the sight when he heard Mr. Matsuo call out to ask whether he was all right. Mr. Matsuo had been safely cushioned within the falling house by the bedding stored in the front hall and had worked his way out. Mr. Tanimoto scarcely answered. He had thought of his wife and baby, his church, his home, his parishioners, all of them down in that awful murk. Once more he began to run in fear—toward the city. (24)

Hersey's method of recording what was thought and said lends great credibility to his narrative, for any dialogue directly quoted would necessarily be a fictionalization since there would have been no way to record the actual words; however, a reporter interviewing the people after the fact could get their memories of their words and ideas.

C. D. B. Bryan tells us that in writing *Friendly Fire*, he was confronted with something of the same problem as was Hersey.

I never wanted to be in this book. I had intended only to be a journalist: unbiased, dispassionate, receptive to all sides. I knew my only chance for articulating the tragedy of [the Vietnam War], the only way I could explain, as I had set out to do, the people's estrangement from their government, their increasing paranoia and distrust, lay in limiting my focus.

By concentrating on one specific incident, the death of Michael Mullen, but restricting myself to this one isolated Iowa farm family's story, I had hoped somehow to encompass the whole. This technique, I later came to recognize, was not a journalist's but a novelist's; and it led inevitably not only to my own participation and inclusion in the Mullen's story but also to that awful sadness and disappointment I now felt. (330)

The amazing accomplishment of *Hiroshima*—in spite of the *TLS* grumping—was the objectivity, even disinterestedness, of the author, letting the facts speak for themselves, which is exactly the reason for much of the praise the book has received through the years. As Ronald Weber says,

Hersey distances himself from his material through impersonal dominance of it. He subjects the material to absolute control. . . . Hersey's personality is never dramatically present, and the "I" is absent entirely; the recording angel always keeps its distance and its mask. But Hersey's sensibility and compassion are deeply felt and the work is finally not only an extraordinary feat of detached reporting but also an experience of great emotional effect. (66)

Bryan wants to achieve both Hersey's documentary credibility— the grounding in verifiable fact—and the novelist's presentational intensity. To accomplish this, Bryan tells us in the "Author's Note," he drew all of his material either from firsthand observation or from "historical texts, public or official records, original correspondence, journals kept by a participant or extended interviews with those persons directly involved" (7). Some of the conversations were, to be sure, "reconstructed," but only on the basis of corroboration by the parties involved or, if necessary, by a third party (7). Bryan wanted the book to be true not only in the general sense of that word, but in the narrow, factual sense.

Authorial presence in the first person, status details, and full dialogue make for the radical difference between *Hiroshima* and *Friendly Fire*. In the following passage from *Friendly Fire*, Michael's father Gene is repairing a television antenna as an Army sergeant and a priest arrive at the farmstead:

He [Gene] buttoned up his heavy woolen red and black lumber jacket, turned off his hearing aid, put the earplug into his pocket and went outside.

The windblown television antenna was attached to a post near the east side of the farmhouse. Gene was just coming around that east corner, blowing hot breath on his fingertips and trying to remember where he had last put the light wrench he would need when, out of the corner of his eye, he noticed two automobiles turning into his driveway. Without his hearing aid he had not heard them approach and he fumbled beneath his lumber jacket for the earpiece, inserted it and thumbed the volume up.

Gene thought he recognized the first car, believed the parish priest, Father Shimon, had one like it, but that second car. . . . Gene read the black letters painted on the olive Chevrolet's drab door: US ARMY—FOR OFFICIAL USE ONLY. Gene's chest tightened, and he stood still while the priest and the Army sergeant stepped out of their cars and slammed shut the doors.

Gene watched them walking toward him as if in slow motion, their footsteps thundering across the metallic crust of the drifted snow. . . . Not until the priest forced himself to look up did Gene recognize the fright, the despair, the agony within them, then very quietly Gene asked, "Is my boy dead?"

Father Shimon halted so abruptly that the Army sergeant, who was following, bumped into him from behind. "Gene," the priest said, "this is Sergeant Fitzgerald. He's from Fifth Army Headquarters. He. . . . " Shimon was silent.

Gene looked beyond Father Shimon to the sergeant and asked again, "Is . . . my . . . boy . . . *dead?*"

"Let's go into the house, Gene," Father Shimon said. "I want to talk to you there."

"No!" Gene said, not moving. "I want to *know!* Tell me, is . . . *my* . . . *boy* . . . *dead?*"

"I can't tell you here," Father Shimon said, his hand fluttering up toward Gene's shoulder. "Come into the house with us . . . please?"

Gene spun away before the priest's pale fingers could touch him. (47–48)

Friendly Fire is a remarkable achievement. As the scene above illustrates, it has all of the dramatic power of a novel; it has the documentary credibility of scrupulous journalism; and, what is more, it embodies a complex argument.

There is no need to quote any of the numerous official documents and personal letters that Bryan includes as what Aristotle would call "inartificial proofs," but his argument needs discussion.

In the first part of the book, we hear the story of Michael Mullen's death from the standpoint of his parents. The boy had been killed in Vietnam by an American artillery round that, through miscalculation, exploded short of its target, over the foxholes of Michael's company. The Mullens were convinced that there had been a cover-up of the facts of the case, which led them more and more deeply into a protest against the whole war. In particular, they accused Michael's battalion commander of misconduct, alleging that his ambition to be promoted made him careless of the lives in his charge. With scrupulous care, Bryan untangles the snarl of charges and responses, of misinterpretations and explanations, of statistics that mean one thing to the Army and another to the Mullens, and he concludes that in the Vietnam tragedy, the truth is neither in the Mullens' bitterness and suspicions nor on the side of the government that embroiled people like the Mullens and their son in a futile war. "It's somewhere in between," Bryan tells the Mullens (330).

In particular, the battalion commander, Lt. Col. H. Norman Schwarzkopf, had come off, in the Mullens' version of events, as an unfeeling, insanely ambitious military automaton, all of the evidence weighing against him; at the end of the book, Schwarzkopf seems to be as tragic a figure as the Mullens themselves, caught up in events that are beyond his control and keenly aware of the moral dilemmas that the Vietnam War created for all caring people who were involved. And Bryan, as a character in his own book, is the compassionate but disinterested commentator. He ends the story of the Mullens' anguish with them in their kitchen. Gene has asked Bryan, "Are we crazy? . . . *Are we?*" Bryan replies with a shake of the head, not sure that he can control his voice. Peg Mullen says that she thinks to herself, "*My God, am I going to be doing this the rest of my life?*"

Finally, after more anguished questioning: " 'Why don't both of you get out of here?' [Peg] asked. 'I'll clean up the breakfast dishes while you two visit Michael's grave' " (335).

It is interesting that Bryan *discovered* himself to be using novelistic techniques to accomplish an "unbiased, dispassionate" end whereas Mailer, to whom we will soon turn, set out to create "a true life novel," allowing himself opportunities that Bryan's contract with the reader precluded. For example, Bryan tells us that on the morning of Michael's death, but forty-eight hours before the family was notified, "Peg had burst into tears for no apparent reason. Off and on that entire day she cried, and so that Gene wouldn't know, she had spent the morning down in the sewing room by herself" (49). This premonitory event is a fact of the story, and Bryan reports it and then drops the theme of psychic awareness. In *The Executioner's Song*, Mailer creates a motif of psychic phenomena and beliefs:

> When their eyes met, Gary looked at her and said, "I know you." Nicole didn't say anything in reply. For a split second, something flashed in her mind but then she thought, No, I've never met him before, I know that. Maybe I know him from another time. (73)

> With her eyes closed, she had the odd feeling of an evil presence near her that came from Gary. She found it kind of half agreeable. She said to herself, Well, if he is the devil, maybe I want to get closer. (106)

> Debbie [the wife of Gilmore's second victim] had been having a strange feeling from Sunday on. It continued all day Monday and was worse on Tuesday afternoon. Same with Ben. (248)

The tone that Bryan establishes in *Friendly Fire* is one of reason; the tone in *The Executioner's Song* is one of premonition and irrationality. Even though Mailer's book is not *about* the irrational (after all, one could have a perfectly rational book about irrationalism, e.g., Lindner's *Fifty-Minute Hour* or Sacks' *The Man Who Mistook His Wife for a Hat*), the author weaves facts and inventions (which we will examine later) into an aura of other-worldliness. Such obvious "artistic" manipulations would have jeopardized the documentary veracity of Bryan's account.

With Michael Herr's *Dispatches*, we enter the realm of *metafiction* (i.e., "works which are organized on the principle of being about themselves" [Hellmann 15]) and leave the world of discursiveness. Herr's book is a series of fragments, some as brief as this one:

> At 800 feet we knew we were being shot at. Something hit the underside of the chopper but did not penetrate it. They weren't firing tracers, but we saw the brilliant flickering blips of light below, and the pilot circled and came down very fast, working the button that released fire from the flex guns mounted on either side of the Huey. Every fifth round was a tracer, and they sailed out and down, incomparably graceful, closer and closer, until they met the tiny point of light coming from the jungle. The ground fire stopped, and we went on to land at Vinh Long, where the pilot yawned and said, "I think I'll go to bed early tonight and see if I can wake up with any enthusiasm for this war." (182)

Though *Dispatches* is not cohesive, one vignette or episode leading syllogistically to the next, it is qualitatively coherent, "adding up" to a work that is unified by theme—the inexplicability of the war—and an attitude of amazed disillusionment, in its unifying force so powerful the reader is hardly aware that structurally the book is a montage.

In a problematic discussion of *The Nonfiction Novel*, Robert Augustin Smart stresses the role of the narrator in the genre, which "requires a subjective, clearly identified narrative perspective different from the unidentified, omniscient perspective of the conventional realistic novel" (3). (By this criterion among others, incidentally, he classes *In Cold Blood* and *The Executioner's Song* as conventional realistic novels.) The author in *Hiroshima* was the anonymous, disinterested, objective reporter, the good journalist; the author in *Friendly Fire* was objective and disinterested, but, like the expository essayist, not anonymous; the author in *Dispatches*, like the author of a confession (e.g., DeQuincey, or Jack Henry Abbott in *In the Belly of the Beast*), is not objective, not disinterested, not anonymous.

The last chapter explained that Herr's book does not count as an argument because its evidence is questionable, and it lacks backing for the link between the evidence and the claim; in fact, it doesn't *assert* in the sense that *Hiroshima* and *Friendly Fire* do, both of which imply their objectivity and empirical validity. With *Dispatches,* we are in the realm of the lyrical, with its scene-agent ratio, act being less important than the attitude danced within and by the work.

It will be recalled that the epigraph with which the second chapter of this book began said, in part, that "the study of lyrical devices might be classed under the head of rhetoric, when these devices are considered for their power to induce or communicate states of mind to readers, even though the kinds of assent evoked have no overt, practical outcome" (Burke, *A Rhetoric of Motives* 50). Communicating a state of mind to readers must have been Herr's intention, but regardless of his original purpose, *that* is what he accomplishes so brilliantly.

Herr, like all poets, is confronting the paradox of unsayability, a fact that he well realizes. And what is a lyric, essentially, but the attempt to say the unsayable? An economic theory can account for wealth, but only a story can explain what it means to be wealthy. The science of aerodynamics explains the flight of a 747, but only a "poem" can convey my exhilaration when I feel the first lift of takeoff and hear the shocks thump to their full extension as the wheels leave the ground.

It is useful here to recall the discussion of Susanne Langer's distinction between *discursive* and *presentational* forms. She says, "I do believe that in this physical, space-time world of our experience there are things which do not fit the grammatical scheme of expression. But they are not necessarily blind, inconceivable, mystical affairs; they are simply matters which require to be conceived through some symbolic schema other than discursive language" (82–83). And the psychologist Endel Tulving's distinction between *verbal* and *episodic* knowledge helps. (As the first chapter of this book explains, the verbal is conceptual, depersonalized: "The formula for table salt is NaCl." But episodic knowledge is biographical, personal, contextualized: "I remember learning the formula for table salt, NaCl, from a dog-eared, navy blue chemistry text during my freshman year in high school. In class, I sat next to Anne Holt and. . . . ")

Perhaps, for a beginning, we can say that the lyric is the residue, the excess, after the discursive, purely verbal element of meaning has been extracted—what remains after "alembification," to use one of Kenneth Burke's favorite terms. Once we have stated and hence removed the thesis of "Sailing to Byzantium," the leftovers are poetry, a kind of knowledge so puzzling that a whole industry labors away to account for it. (No Fermi Lab for this gigantic enterprise, of course.)

In Herr's lyrical reports on the Vietnam War, reason counts little and impression much; hard data is not as important as image and intuition.

There wasn't a day when someone didn't ask me what I was doing there. Sometimes an especially smart grunt or another correspondent would even ask me what I was *really* doing there, as though I could say anything honest about it except "Blah blah blah cover the war" or "Blah blah blah write a book." . . . The problem was that you didn't always know what you were seeing until later, maybe years later, that a lot of it never made it in at all, it just stayed stored in your eyes. Time and information, rock and roll, life itself, the information isn't frozen, you are.

Sometimes I didn't know if an action took a second or an hour or if I dreamed it or what. In war more than in other life you don't really know what you're doing most of the time, you're just behaving, and afterwards you can make up any kind of bullshit you want to about it, say you felt good and bad, loved it or hated it, did this or that, the right thing or the wrong thing; still, what happened happened. (19–20)

In spite of all this puzzlement and self doubt, there remains the specificity and tangibility of concrete images, the real substance of lyric poetry:

When the 173rd held services for their dead from Dak To the boots of the dead men were arranged in formation on the ground. It was an old paratrooper tradition, but knowing that didn't reduce it or make it any less spooky, a company's worth of jump boots standing empty in the dust taking benediction, while the real substance of the ceremony was being bagged and tagged and shipped back home through what they called the KIA Travel Bureau. (23)

Dispatches reaches the limits of what can be "said" with language and strains beyond them. The next step is the one that Agee took in *Let Us Now Praise Famous Men:* pictures supplementing the words. And beyond that? The silent language of pictures.

Finally, it must be said that the focus on *agent*—on ethical appeal—in the discussion of *Hiroshima, Friendly Fire,* and *Dispatches* necessarily minimized *pathos* or persuasion. A second "reading" of the texts from the standpoint of *pathos* could fill in the gaps left by the analysis from the standpoint of *ethos,* but rather than map a new course through familiar territory, we will move on.

Pathos and the Confession

" 'You know, Norman,' said [Robert] Lowell in his fondest voice, 'Elizabeth and I really think you're the finest journalist in America' " (Mailer, *Armies* 32). This compliment sets Mailer off on a train of ungenerous thoughts, until Lowell says again, "'Yes, Norman, I really think you are the best journalist in America'" (33), to which Mailer responds, " 'Well, Cal . . . there are days when I think of myself as being the best writer in America' " (33). Lowell generously and embarrassedly apologizes for his gaffe: " 'Oh, Norman, oh, certainly . . . I didn't mean to imply, heavens no, it's just I have such *respect* for good journalism' " (33).

Whether or not Mailer is the best writer in America, he ranks as a journalist only if the qualifying adjective "new" precedes the

"journalist," and even then I believe that *Armies of the Night* belongs
to a category of literature outside journalism, old or new (though
Miami and the Siege of Chicago is in). *Armies* is "subjective, creative,
and candid," the qualities that according to Michael L. Johnson set
new journalism apart from old (xi), but in its semantic intention,
the book is nearer to the confessions of Augustine, Rousseau, and
DeQuincey than it is to *The Kandy-Kolored Tangerine-Flake Streamline
Baby* or *The Algiers Motel Incident*. Both Norman and Jean-Jacques
are driven by ego, revealing themselves (or a persona, and in principle it makes no difference which) with a candor that "confesses" to
great ability, to genius, as well as to baseness. Here is Rousseau:

> Let the trumpet of the day of judgement sound when it will, I shall
> appear with this book in my hand before the Sovereign Judge, and cry with
> a loud voice, This is my work, these were my thoughts, and thus was I. I
> have freely told both the good and the bad, have hid nothing wicked, added
> nothing good; and if I have happened to make use of an insignificant
> ornament, it was only to fill a void occasioned by a short memory: I may
> have supposed true what I knew might be so, never what I knew was false.
> I have exposed myself as I was, contemptible and vile some times; at others,
> good, generous, and sublime. I have revealed my heart as thou sawest it
> thyself. Eternal Being! assemble around me the numberless throng of my
> fellow-mortals; let them listen to my Confessions, let them lament my
> unworthiness, let them blush at my misery. Let each of them, in his turn,
> lay open his heart with the same sincerity at the foot of thy throne, and
> then say, if he dare, *I was better than that man.* (3–4)

And here Mailer:

> Mailer had a complex mind of sorts. Like a later generation which was to
> burn holes in their brain on Speed, he had given his own head the texture
> of a fine Swiss cheese. Years ago he had made all sorts of erosions in his
> intellectual firmament by consuming modestly promiscuous amounts of
> whiskey, marijuana, seconal, and benzedrine. It had given him the illusion
> he was a genius, as indeed an entire generation of children would so come
> to see themselves a decade later out on celestial journeys of LSD. (15)

Or take the resemblance between the addict DeQuincey and the
dipsomaniac Mailer, which is more than the accident of their de-
pendencies; they are brother confessionalists because of their self-
absorption. It occurs to neither that the world at large will be unin-

terested in their solipsistic, hazy excursions through history—and they are perfectly right in this assumption.

In the confession, the focus is sharply on the author *in propria persona* as he or she goes through a central experience (of conversion, disillusionment, enlightenment, etc.). How, one might ask, do I make a clear distinction between autobiography and confession? My answer: "I don't." However, one can imagine that an autobiography—Eisenhower's *At Ease,* for instance, or *The Education of Henry Adams*—is written for what Perelman and Olbrechts-Tyteca call "the universal audience" (31–35), which is not an actual group of readers, but an idealized readership that is perfectly rational and disinterested, wanting those qualities to be obvious in the author's semantic intention. "Philosophers always claim to be addressing such an audience, not because they hope to obtain the effective assent of all men—they know very well that only a small minority will ever read their works—but because they think that all who understand the reasons they give will have to accept their conclusions" (31). An autobiography can be impersonal; a confession cannot.

From the time *Armies* first appeared, there was confusion over its genre. In *Book World* (April 28, 1968), Mario Puzo (accurately, in my opinion) said that "The book as a whole [is] mostly a character study of Mailer and as such crueler than the classic Lillian Ross profile of Hemingway." Alfred Kazin sees the book also as a "confession" (my term, of course, not his):

I believe that *Armies of the Night* is just as brilliant a personal testimony as Whitman's diary of the Civil War, "Specimen Days," and Whitman's great essay on the crisis of the Republic during the Gilded Age, "Democratic Vistas." I believe that it is a work of personal and political reportage that brings to the inner and developing crisis of the United States at this moment admirable sensibilities, candid intelligence, the most moving concern for America itself. Mailer's intuition in this book is that the times demand a new form. He has found it. (1)

On the other hand, Josh Greenfield sees in *Armies* "as complete and thoroughgoing an account as one could hope for" and H. S. Resnik thinks it is "probably the truest picture we have of what has been happening to America . . . [combining] the objectivity of journalism and the intimacy of a memoir."

Zavarzadeh calls *Armies* a "testimonial nonfiction novel," which is "the narrative of encounter between the author—the historical person whose name appears on the title page, not a fictional 'second self '—and the brute psychic or physical facts" (130). The term "testimonial" is all to the good, but, as I will argue, "nonfiction novel" is inappropriate.

When compared with *Hiroshima, Friendly Fire,* and even *Dispatches,* however, *Armies* appears monomaniacal, uninformative about the segment of history it ostensibly reports, and extraordinarily idiosyncratic. It is pretty clearly a classic, for the community of readers has bestowed value upon it, yet I would argue that it is a less satisfactory work than the three classics dealt with earlier in this chapter.

The Rhetoric of Metarhetoric

It will be recalled that at one point C. D. B. Bryan resorted to what the current jargon calls "metadiscourse," i.e., discourse about discourse; he discovered that the technique he had chosen—"concentrating on one specific incident, the death of Michael Mullen"—turned out to be the technique of a novelist, not that of a journalist. Michael Herr also lapsed into "metadiscourse" when he wrote of the "uni-prose which all news magazines and papers maintained" (226), getting all the facts but never finding "a way to report meaningfully about death, which of course was really what it was all about" (229). Mailer goes beyond metadiscourse to what might be called "metarhetoric," continually attempting to persuade the reader that his method is not only valid, but the only way to get at the truth of his subject.

Mailer must convince us that his *method* is right so that he can convince us that his *attitude* is right.

This problem is, of course, not unique to Norman Mailer, but seems unavoidable for the writer of confessions. Rousseau's first sentence is "I am undertaking a work which has no example, and whose execution will have no imitator." In the first chapter of the eleventh book Augustine justifies writing his *Confessions:* "O Lord, since eternity is Thine, art Thou ignorant of the things which I say unto Thee? Or seest Thou at the time that which cometh to pass in time? Why, therefore, do I place before Thee so many relations of things? Not surely that Thou mighest know them through me, but that I may awaken my own love and that of my readers towards

Thee, that we may all say, 'Great is the Lord, and greatly to be praised.'"

James Agee's problem in *Let Us Now Praise Famous Men*—also a confession—is simply this: to present his vision of reality in such a way that readers will accept its truth, exactly the same problem that confronted Norman Mailer in *The Armies of the Night*.

> The nominal subject is North American cotton tenantry as examined in the daily living of three representative white tenant families.
>
> Actually, the effort is to recognize the stature of a portion of unimagined existence, and to contrive techniques proper to its recording, communication, analysis, and defense. More essentially, this is an independent inquiry into certain normal predicaments of human divinity. (xiv)

Form, genre—whatever one calls it, shaping his materials must have been excruciatingly difficult for Agee. (Or perhaps the form simply came, and the pain was in justifying what had been given.) The book starts with sixty-one photographs by Walker Evans, "reproduced through the courtesy of the Farm Security Administration, United States Department of Agriculture." The preface, which follows the photographs (after a note on Agee by Evans), explains that *Let Us Now Praise Famous Men* is one volume of a larger work, to be titled *Three Tenant Families*, and that it is "a *book* only by necessity" (xvi). "More seriously, it is an effort in human actuality, in which the reader is no less centrally involved than the authors and those of whom they tell" (xvi). And to create the ultimate nonartistic work, Agee invites readers to participate in the subject, "in whatever degree of understanding, friendship, or hostility" by writing to the authors in care of the publisher (xvi).

Book One consists of five pages that include: (1) a quotation from *King Lear*. (2) The slogan "Workers of the world, unite and fight. You have nothing to lose but your chains, and a world to win," followed by a footnote explaining that the slogan does not imply the authors' commitment to "any political party, faith, or faction" (xix). (3) A page from a third-grade geography textbook, about the human need for food, shelter, and clothing. (4) "Persons and Places," a rundown of relationships among the tenant farmers and minimal data about the scenes in which they live.

The structure of Book Two is equally idiosyncratic, as the following from pages 2 and 3 indicates:

DESIGN OF BOOK TWO

Like Mailer, Agee was writing "fact," not "fiction," and that posed enormous difficulties, for since Aristotle, we have known that fiction is more veracious than history; that fact-based texts are mere journalism; that journalism only copies, doesn't create. Hence both Mailer and Agee elaborately justified their resorting to fact when fiction is the proper realm of the serious writer.

Better than halfway through his book, Agee breaks into a paean on art. It is both better and worse than science because it makes dangerous and even impossible bargains "and makes the best of it, becoming, as a result, both nearer the truth and farther from it" than science and scientific art, which merely describe (238). (In other words, art is better than science because it results from the creative powers of the secondary imagination.) However, the necessity for a willing suspension of disbelief in regard to art means that "anything set forth within an art form . . . is hermetically sealed away from identification with everyday 'reality' " (240).

In the meantime,

George Gudger is a man, et cetera. But obviously, in the effort to tell of him (by example) as truthfully as I can, I am limited. I know him only so far as I know him, and only in those terms in which I know him; and all of that depends as fully on who I am as on who he is.

I am confident of being able to get at a certain form of the truth about him, *only if* I am as faithful as possible to Gudger as I know him, to Gudger as, in his actual flesh and life (but there again always in my mind's and memory's eye) he is. But of course it will only be a relative truth. (239)

One feels that Agee *knew* he had a moral, human obligation to create what we have called presentational nonfiction, but a professional obligation to write fiction. Because of the importance of his subject, because a character in the book "*exists,* in actual being, as you do and as I do, and as no character of imagination can possibly exist," the writing about this character will have more immediacy than fiction could possibly achieve, "a kind of meaning, not at all necessarily 'superior' to that of imagination, but of a kind so different that a work of the imagination (however intensely it may draw on 'life') can at best only faintly imitate the least of it" (12). What, after all, could be superior to the meaning that results from the creative powers of the imagination?

Then the ultimate *meta*-confession: "If I could do it, I'd do no writing at all here. It would be photographs; the rest would be fragments of cloth, bits of cotton, lumps of earth, records of speech, pieces of wood and iron, phials of odors, plates of food and of excrement" (13). Agee knew that in his purpose, he was reaching the borders of the sayable, but also, bitterly, that nearing those borders and trying to cross them would alienate him from his possible audience: "Booksellers would consider it quite a novelty; critics would murmur, yes, but is it art; and I could trust a majority of you to use it as you would a parlor game" (13). In fact, he must have been speaking not of his imagined "concrete" book, but of *Let Us Now Praise Famous Men.*

Book One of *Armies,* 241 pages, is "History as Novel: The Steps of the Pentagon," but a strange novel indeed if one compares it with a "conventional" fiction such as, say, *Humboldt's Gift* or a "conventional" nonfiction novel such as *The Executioner's Song.* The energy that propels a reader through the book comes not from plot, not from the desire for information, but from that critical mass, Norman Mailer's ego. Calling it a novel collapses the useful distinctions among confession, autobiography, and nonfiction novel.

Rhetor, Rhetorician

In *Armies,* Mailer is more the rhetor and the rhetorician than in any of his other works. We see him as failed orator and as metarhetorician.

The Failed Orator. It is easy enough to conjure a metaphysical reason for the egomaniacal incoherence of Mailer's speech in the Ambassador Theater, and Chris Anderson has done just that, implying that Rhetor Mailer is reacting against "step-by-step, careful, programmatic expression," which is "not only stylistically uninteresting but finally useless" (100). Here is a sample of Mailer's counter-style:

"What are you, dead-heads?" he bellowed at the audience. "Or are you all"—here he put on his false Irish accent—"in the nature of becoming dead ahsses?" Small laughs. A whistle or two. "No," he said, replying to the whistles, "I invoke these dead asses as part of the gravity of the occasion. The middle class plus one hippie surrealistic symbolic absolutely insane March on the Pentagon, bless us all," beginning of a big applause which offended Mailer for it came on "bless" and that was too cheap a way to win votes, "bless us all—shit!" he shouted. "I'm trying to say the middle class plus shit, I mean plus revolution, is equal to one big collective dead ass." Some yells of approval, but much shocked curious rather stricken silence. He had broken the shank of his oratorical charge. Now he would have to sweep the audience together again. (Perhaps he felt like a surgeon delivering a difficult breech—nothing to do but plunge to the elbows again.) (50)

Ultimately, after some altercation about who should be master of ceremonies, Mailer relinquishes the stage to Robert Lowell for poetry reading, Lowell the patrician: "One did not achieve the languid grandeurs of that slouch in one generation" (57). Genteel, slightly effete, tweedy Robert Lowell angers burly, profane Norman Mailer, for Lowell, who is as inept a speaker as Mailer, finally wins the accolade that was denied Mailer. The crowd "adored him—for his talent, his modesty, his superiority, his melancholy, his petulance, his weakness, his painful, almost stammering shyness, his noble strength" (58). And Mailer, even though he was "a bulldog about the value of his own talent" (58), discovered that he was jealous.

Of course, we can trust Mailer, perhaps even more than we can trust Lowell, whose patrician reticence might well prevent him from being completely and spontaneously honest in the way that is apparently characteristic of Mailer, whose candor about his failure as an orator has built his credibility as a historian.

As orator, of course, Mailer was doomed because a perfectly valid theory of *written* composition failed him. He briefly states a principle that both rhetorical theory and empirical research substantiate: writing (usually) is a process of integrating opportunities and discoveries into an overall semantic intention (e.g., Flower and Hayes 1979), which is exactly what Mailer says: "Consider that a good half of writing consists of being sufficiently sensitive to the moment to reach for the next promise which is usually hidden in some word or phrase just a shift to the side of one's conscious intent" (40). Public speaking, however, is, in Mailer's view, cut-and-dried, uninspired and uninspiring, "a sullen expression of human possibility metaphorically equal to a bugger on his victim" (40). What Mailer has forgotten, of course, is that as a writer he has a "conscious intent," a general goal. As a speaker, he decides to "wing it," beginning with no particular semantic intention and letting inspiration and his own personality carry him *to* one. However, as John Madden says of some football fans, Mailer has only one oar in the water, and he goes in circles, much to the disgust of the audience.

The Metarhetorician. The second, shorter part of *Armies,* Book Two, titled "The Novel as History: The Battle of the Pentagon," begins as the work of a sober, prudent observer-commentator (Norman Mailer as George Wills), not at all the moody, loud, boozy shouter or mumbler of the first part. On the first page of Book Two, Mailer tells us that the first 241 pages have been a microscopic view of events, just the sort of narrative best accomplished by the novel, not a panorama, but a series of portraits. In the second book, however, Mailer will become the historian, viewing events from a tower through a telescope (though with an inevitably warped lens).

For the next thirty-nine pages, Mailer decorously provides chronicle and commentary, the only incongruity being the chapter titles, which, in fact, foreshadow an inevitable breakdown: 2. Symbolic Search, 3. Cautionary Crafts, 4. An Arbitrated Aesthetic, 5. A Perspective of Battle, and 6. A Palette of Tactics.

In the sixth chapter, finally, Mailer must *admit* that since "an explanation of the mystery of the events at the Pentagon cannot be developed by the methods of history," he will "now unashamedly enter that world of strange lights and intuitive speculation which is the novel" (284), not because he chooses to fictionalize, but because novelistic techniques are the only methods that will enable him, and through him his readers, to comprehend the virtually incomprehensible.

Shelley Fisher Fishkin reports that John Hersey "believes —passionately—that 'a great deal of harm has been done in recent years by the notion that something *can* be both a novel and journalism at the same time' " (208). In a *Yale Review* article, Hersey had challenged some of the supposed facts in *The Executioner's Song*, but in a Yale seminar taught by Fishkin, Mailer said that he had been meticulously accurate on the points that Hersey questioned. However, on the same occasion "he also confessed to having largely invented several other parts of the book ('The stuff on April, the sister of Nicole, is probably three-quarters fanciful . . . I'd say it was ninety-five percent fictional, in fact, with April . . .')" (208). In his conflation of fact and fiction, Mailer seems to be saying with Socrates, in the *Phaedrus*, that factual knowledge is often boorish wisdom, the truth lying not in historicity, but in mythic significance.

In genre, *Armies* is as iconoclastic as *Let Us Now Praise Famous Men*, both of which claim truth, but not factuality. If readers accept Agee's and Mailer's metarhetoric concerning form, the books will be persuasive. Obviously, both authors were successful.

CHAPTER 4
Logos: Journalism and Dramatic Exposition

A false truth can offer more reality than the truth that was altered.

—Norman Mailer, *Marilyn*

If it's information you want, go to the *Encyclopaedia Britannica.*

—Old English department saying

A chapter on the "new journalism," which is almost obligatory in a book about "the literature of fact," will complete the survey of types of arguments. *Ethos* and *pathos* gave chapter 3 its orientation; *logos* is the basis for this chapter.

It is a commonly held view that the literature of fact, the nonfiction novel, the new journalism—these overlapping, chimerical categories—have their origins in a crisis: the inability of traditional genres to represent a reality that has become increasingly enigmatic. Hellmann can be the spokesperson for the critics holding this point of view, including Weber (9), Zavarzadeh (3–49), Wolfe ("The New Journalism" 28), Johnson (xi-xvi), and others.:

The basic assumption of nineteenth-century fiction, like that of twentieth-century journalism, lay in the existence of an objective reality that could be simply recorded. But for most Americans in the 1960s, perhaps the central reality was that everyday life now involved implausible characters and events delivered into the home by the media. The realm of the believable had become an extremely doubtful concept. (9)

Though I have no intention of trying to explain the phylogeny of nonfiction literature, attributing mutations strictly to a change in the sensibilities of the readership probably oversimplifies a complex

of circumstances involving at the very least a political struggle between academic arbiters of taste, who at the vanguard were valuing
a postmodernism that was outside the interests of the "common
reader," and the nonacademic journalists, whose work seemed more
and more like that great democratic art form the realistic novel. As
I was reading over the first chapter of *The Great Tradition,* a manifesto that I suppose is now largely forgotten, it occurred to me
that new journalism is the extension of the tradition and that the
postmodernist novel is the dead end of formalist experimentation
that Leavis predicted. In any case, new journalism is for serious
nonacademic readers in the last half of the twentieth century what
the great realistic novel was to nineteenth-century readership. As
Norman Podhoretz said in "The Article as Art," the magazine article
is more appropriate than fiction as an art form for the age.

The new journalism genre—if one can call it that, though perhaps
"movement" is a better term—can be traced to a group of feature
writers associated with *Esquire,* the *New York Herald Tribune,* and
other publications (Wolfe, "The New Journalism" 3–9) and to writers for the underground press of the 1960s (Johnson 3–22). (Wolfe
mentions Charles Portis, Jimmy Breslin, Dick Schaap, Gay Talese,
Robert Lipsyste, and Michael Mok.) I have no revisionist theories
about the history of what is called the new journalism, nor do I
choose to join the argument over the esthetics of the works thus
classified. Hellmann says flatly that the new journalism is fiction.
Thus, for example, Styron writing about Nat Turner, events from
the chronicle of the past, created a historical novel; Mailer writing
about the march on the Pentagon, events of the moment, created
fiction as new journalism. In Wolfe's view, the new journalism, using
the novelist's techniques and the reporter's meticulousness and energy, creates a more penetrating view of reality.

A crucial part of Breslin's work they [the literary intellectuals] didn't seem
to be conscious of at all: namely, the reporting he did. Breslin made it a
practice to arrive on the scene long before the main event in order to gather
the off-camera material, the by-play in the make-up room, that would
enable him to create character. It was part of his *modus operandi* to gather
"novelistic" details, the rings, the perspiration, the jabs on the shoulder,
and he did it more skillfully than most novelists. (14)

James E. Murphy's brief characterization of the new journalism
is quite adequate for our purposes: "It is an artistic, creative, literary

reporting form with three basic traits: dramatic literary techniques; intensive reporting; and reporting of generally acknowledged subjectivity" (16).

This chapter, centered not so firmly on the psychology of information, will begin with John McPhee (*Rising from the Plains*), a master literary craftsman whose work is endlessly engaging; inquiring about the *rhetoric* of information, the discussion will then peregrinate from this enormously successful author to *The Right Stuff*, which in my view is superb literature. The chapter will end with a work that represents the decadence of the new journalism, *The Curse of Lono*, by Hunter S. Thompson.

John McPhee and the Craft of Writing

In his introduction to *The John McPhee Reader*, William L. Howarth gives an interesting and useful account of John McPhee's method of composition, which can fairly be summarized as gathering and arranging: taking copious notes (in the field, from interviews, from library resources), arranging the notes (according to either "mechanic" or "organic" principles), and then writing the successive drafts of his works. Since it is the result of logic, McPhee prefers the "mechanic" form, "but he trusts the organic principle enough not to condone formal manipulation for its own sake. Too much shuffling of those cards leads to fussy and baroque patterns, reflecting the self-indulgent mind of their maker" (xxii).

McPhee's genius is his ability to use a narrative structure as a vehicle for conveying facts and judgments, a rhetorical technique characteristic of good journalism.

Rising from the Plains, McPhee's third book concerning geology (along with *Basin and Range* and *In Suspect Terrain*, part of the series titled *Annals of the Former World*), in its 214 pages gives a synecdochic history of frontier Wyoming, a portrait of a modern Wyoming geologist, and a survey of the geology of the Rocky Mountains, the three disparate themes woven into a seamless whole, centering on the biography and professional concerns of the geologist, David Love, scion of a pioneer Wyoming family. McPhee begins the book with a candid explanation of what he is going to do: "This is about high-country geology and a Rocky Mountain regional geologist. I raise that semaphore here at the start so no one will feel misled by an opening passage in which a slim young woman who is not in any sense a geologist steps down from a train in Rawlins, Wyoming, in order to go north by stagecoach into country that was still very much the Old West" (3). As we learn later, Miss Ethel Waxham arrived in Rawlins in 1905 when she was twenty-three, a blond, Phi Beta Kappa graduate of Wellesley, on her way to the Red Bluff Ranch, in the vicinity of which she would be mistress of the one-room school on Twin Creek near the mouth of Skull Gulch, her job "to deliver a hundred per cent of the formal education available in District Eleven, Fremont County, Wyoming" (30). Sixty miles from the Red Bluff Ranch lived a nephew of John Muir, John Love, an adventurer who came west from Wisconsin to be a cowboy.

Through the eighteen-nineties, there are various hiatuses in the résumé of John Love, but as cowboy and homesteader he very evidently prospered, and he also formed durable friendships—with Chief Washakie, for example, and with the stagecoach driver Peggy Dougherty, and with Robert LeRoy Parker and Harry Longabaugh (Butch Cassidy and the Sundance Kid). There came a day when Love could not contain his developed curiosity in the presence of the aging chief. He asked him what truth there was in the story of Crowheart Butte. Had Washakie really eaten his enemy's heart? The chief said, "Well, Johnny, when you're young and full of life you do strange things." (37–38)

John Love, of course, married Ethel Waxham, and they became the parents of David Love, "supervisor of the [United States Geological] Survey's environmental branch in Laramie, and—to an extent un-usual at the highest levels of the science—an autochthonous geolo-gist" (4), that is, a geologist whose specialty is rock that has not moved.

The story of Ethel Waxham Love and her husband John is a marvelous representative anecdote of frontier life and people: an American fable. The sections of the book that deal with David Love could be removed and used, *mutatis mutandis,* as a *New Yorker* profile. Finally, the discussions of geology are perfect examples of their kind: clear expositions of scientific fact for lay readers.

McPhee's books are always informative, whether the subject is oranges (as in *Oranges*) or the Swiss army (as in *La Place de la Concorde Suisse*); as Howarth points out, the narrative centers on an interesting "hero" such as David Love; and the works are rich in the texture of concrete detail ("He [Love] has had the same old U.S.G.S. air mattress for forty years. When it was quite new, it sprang a leak. He poured evaporated milk in through the valve and stopped the leak" [6].) No writing could be more appropriately readable than McPhee's; the structure of his expository narrative is brilliant. In short, McPhee creates superb *discursive* literature, discursive because (1) the "drama" serves the purposes of exposition; (2) the speaker in the books, like the speaker in *Hiroshima*, is neutral, his attitudes *not* dancing; (3) in the trade-off between texture and accessibility, McPhee largely opts for accessibility; (4) the author-reader "contract," set up by his metadiscourse, promises discursiveness.

McPhee's dramatistic strategy might, somewhat disingenuously, be characterized as humanizing geology by making that subject a central element in the portrait of one character and his history, but surely the semantic intention behind the book is more complex than this, for as we read, we sense that the author is as interested in the representative anecdote of Love and his history as in the facts of geology that are the ostensible expository focus of *Rising from the Plains*. Yet David Love the geologist does not emerge as a "rounded" character as does Gary Gilmore or Perry Smith, whom we get to know in all of their enigmatic complexity as killers, dreamers, family members, with the whole range of human desires and feelings.

It is no criticism of *Rising from the Plains* to say that Love does not become "rounded"; McPhee's central character serves the purposes of exposition admirably and would not do so if readers were interested primarily in the *drama* rather than the information that the drama is intended to convey.

As we have noted, Kenneth Burke characterizes the lyric ratio as that of agent-scene, the agent being both the author and a character in the drama, perhaps the only character. Throughout his work, McPhee almost never emerges as a character in his own right, though he appears now and then as craftsman, as the maker of the piece—for example, at the beginning of *Rising from the Plains*, where he explains to readers what he is going to do. This absence is an important factor in the reader's response to the book as a piece of discursive writing, for the writer as reporter, not as participant, maintains a rhetorical stance of objectivity and aloofness that is impossible otherwise. To be sure, the reportorial stance is only one factor in the book's being taken as discursive, and certainly the stance of Norman Mailer in *The Executioner's Song* (as opposed to *The Armies of the Night*) or that of Truman Capote in *In Cold Blood* is similar to McPhee's in *Rising from the Plains*, which is only to say that the difference between presentational and discursive literature depends on multiple factors, not merely one.

McPhee opts for elegantly straightforward prose, the kind of lucidity that validates fact. By way of contrast, consider the "voice" speaking in the following passage from *Dispatches:*

Because the Highlands of Vietnam are spooky, unbearably spooky, spooky beyond belief. They are a run of erratic mountain ranges, gnarled valleys, jungled ravines and abrupt plains where Montagnard villages cluster, thin and disappear as the terrain steepens. The Montagnards in all of their tribal components make up the most primitive and mysterious portion of the Vietnamese population, a population that has always confused Americans even in its most Westernized segments. Strictly speaking, the Montagnards are not really Vietnamese at all, certainly not *South* Vietnamese, but a kind of upgraded, demi-enlightened Annamese aborigine, often living in nakedness and brooding silence in their villages. (Herr 99)

This prose—with its repetition of "spooky," its highly cumulative syntax, its adjectives ("erratic," "gnarled," "abrupt")—calls attention to itself and to the partisan passions of the speaker, thus tending to diminish the value of *logos* and to move away from discursiveness and toward presentation.

And here is McPhee:

In the western outskirts of Rawlins, David Love pulled over onto the shoulder of the interstate, the better to fix the scene, although his purpose in doing so was not at all apparent. Rawlins reposed among low hills and prairie flats, and nothing in its setting would ever lift the stock of Eastman Kodak. In those western outskirts, we may have been scarcely a mile from the county courthouse, but we were very much back on the range—a dispassionate world of bare rock, brown grass, drab green patches of greasewood, and scattered colonies of sage. The interstate had lithified in 1965 as white concrete but was now dark with the remains of ocean algae, cremated and sprayed on the road. To the south were badlands—gullies and gulches, erosional debris. To the north were some ridgelines that ended sharply like breaking waves, but the Rawlins Uplift had miserably fallen short in its bid to be counted among the Rocky Mountains. So why was David Love, who had the geologic map of Wyoming in his head, stopping here? (22–23)

This passage is typical of McPhee's prose: easy and lucid— elegant, one might say—and enlivened by specific, sometimes idiosyncratic, detail (such as the remarks about the lithified highway now sprayed with asphalt). One searches uneasily for the proper vocabulary, terms that will characterize both Herr and McPhee without downgrading either. Perhaps one could say that the slight opacity of Herr's prose and the total lucidity of McPhee's are ideal for these writers' purposes. Multiple signals alert the reader to the contract offered by McPhee. The endpapers of the Farrar, Straus, Giroux edition of *Rising from the Plains* are geological charts of the cenozoic and mesozoic eras. From the blurb on the flaps of the jacket, we learn that the book is about geology and "the life of a geologist born in the center of Wyoming and raised on an isolated ranch." And the first sentence of the book declares, "This is about high-country geology and a Rocky Mountain regional geologist" (3). The psychology of information is evoked, and the reader, with the help of the writer, constructs a discursive text.

In any case, *Rising from the Plains* is clearly worth contemplating for its own sake, aside from its informativeness, and I would venture the guess that it, as part of the McPhee oeuvre, will be permanent. It is literature of very high quality.

The Taming of Tom Wolfe

Tom Wolfe's highly mannered earlier work liberated serious journalism from its gray respectability and created the possibility of highly idiosyncratic reporting. Not only were Wolfe's titles calculated as shibboleths of freedom from traditional genre restraints, but his prose was as radical in its way as was the new music of the 1950s and 1960s. Here, for instance, is the beginning of "Las Vegas (What?) Las Vegas (Can't hear you! Too noisy) Las Vegas!!!"

Hernia, hernia, hernia, hernia, hernia, hernia, hernia, hernia, hernia, hernia, hernia, hernia, hernia, HERNia; hernia, HERNia, hernia, hernia, hernia, hernia, HERNia, HERNia, HERNia, hernia, hernia, hernia, hernia, hernia, hernia, hernia, eight is the point, the point is eight; hernia, hernia, HERNia; hernia, hernia, hernia, all right, hernia, hernia, hernia, hernia, hard eight, hernia, hernia, hernia, HERNia, hernia, hernia, hernia, HER-Nia, hernia, hernia, hernia, HERNia, hernia, hernia, hernia, hernia.
"What is all this *hernia hernia* stuff?"
This was Raymond talking to the wavy-haired fellow with the stick, the dealer, at the craps table about 3:45 Sunday morning. (*Kandy* 3)

This stuff was lively, new. In a review of *The Pump House Gang* and *The Electric Kool-Aid Acid Test*, Robert Scholes had said that "The

so-called stylistic excesses of such men as Norman Mailer and Tom
Wolfe are in my view no more than indispensable equipment they
must employ in doing justice to our times. This is not to say that
one must himself be hysterical to chronicle hysteria, but to suggest
that hysteria cannot be assimilated and conveyed by one who is
totally aloof" (37). Scholes suggests that Wolfe and Mailer are "hyst-
orians" who must operate differently from conventional journalists.
Nonetheless, I think that if Wolfe had not attempted more than
"hystory," he would have consigned himself to that literary demi-
monde inhabited by such oners as John Lyly, Ronald Firbanks,
James Branch Cabell, and Djuna Barnes, figures who glitter briefly
and then fizzle, remembered, if at all, as curious sports and evidence
of how far astray taste can go.

   With *The Right Stuff*, a superb literary work, Wolfe established
himself as a mainstream author.

   This book is not a radical departure from young Tom Wolfe,
l'enfant terrible of American letters, but an evolutionary development. A hallmark of Wolfe's style has always been the lapse from
straight exposition into hypothetical dialogue, as in the following
from "The Last American Hero":

[T]hey [the revenuers] had the barricades up and they could hear this
souped-up car roaring around the bend, and here it comes—but suddenly
they can hear a siren and see a red light flashing in the grille, so they think
it's another agent, and boy, they run out like ants and pull those barrels
and boards and sawhorses out of the way, and then—Ggghhzzzzzzz-
hhhhhhgggggg zzzzzzzeeeeeong!—gawdam! there he goes again, it was
him, Junior Johnson! with a gawdam agent's si-reen and a red light in his
grille! (*Kandy* 29)

In *The Right Stuff*, Wolfe lucidly and calmly outlines the stages of a
Navy pilot's training, the ultimate being carrier landings. In this
passage, we again find the switch from third person exposition to
the monologue of a character:

The first day was always a clear day with little wind and a calm sea. The
carrier was so steady that it seemed, from up there in the air, to be resting on
pilings, and the candidate usually made his first carrier landing successfully,
with relief and even *élan*. . . . In the training film the flight deck was a grand
piece of gray geometry, perilous, to be sure, but an amazing abstract shape
as one looks down upon it on the screen. And yet once the newcomer's two
feet were on it . . . *Geometry*—my God, man, this is a . . . skillet. (26)

The question, of course, is why a reader would put *The Right Stuff* in the subgenre with *Rising from the Plains*—as new journalism— rather than with *The Executioner's Song*, as a nonfiction novel, and the straightforward answer is that, like the McPhee book, Wolfe's dramatization of the Mercury project and its astronauts gains its power *largely* from the psychology of information. First and most obviously, the book, like all good exposition, *tells* more than it *shows*. Second, the characters in *The Right Stuff* are no more "rounded" than is John Love; we learn few "incidental" details about them. Just as we have no sense of David Love's home life, his passions aside from geology, and so on, so we get very few "status" details concerning the astronauts. For example, Wolfe gives a fascinating account of the tensions and factions that built up among the astro-nauts, particularly those resulting from John Glenn's Puritanical attitudes. In this account, Wolfe explains the situation and gives us those details that help make the point, but not the richness of specificity that brings characters and scenes to life in *stories*.

> Grissom and Slayton somewhat dourly sided with Glenn on this particular point. Since he was making such a federal case out of it, they would acknowledge the soundness of his logic. But this didn't mean they idolized him any more than Schirra or Shepherd did. A basic division was building up in the group. It was the other five against the pious fair-haired boy and his sidekick, Carpenter. Some of them seemed to derive some satisfaction from lumping Carpenter with Glenn. What was Carpenter even doing here! They couldn't get over the fact that Scott and his wife, Rene, had flamboyant cushions on the floor of their living room and they actually sat there while Scott played the guitar and Rene sang. The fact that she had a trained voice made no difference. It was beatnik stuff. Not only that, Carpenter was a great pal of the doctors. He and Glenn were both like that. They went out of their way to cooperate with the Life Sciences people, too. (175)

In *Style as Argument,* Chris Anderson argues that throughout his work Wolfe is concerned with the limits of language, with attempt-ing to say the unsayable (8–47). In *The Right Stuff,* says Anderson, "the underlying issue is the inexplicability of the experience Wolfe is trying to describe" (13) This, it seems to me, is a misinterpretation. Compared with that other masterful study of astronautics, Mailer's *Of a Fire on the Moon,* we have the feeling that Wolfe was able to find the discursive means to express his complete semantic intention— insofar as that is possible in any kind of language. Anderson says that the rhetorical problem is the distinction "between the actual experience of the right stuff—of being a fighter pilot and experiencing, for example, night landings on an aircraft carrier—and any prior effort to describe that experience in language" (13). Granted, it is difficult to convey the experience of any physical act or sensation in natural language, which is exactly the point about the difference between presentational and discursive writing; however, Wolfe's *motif* is not the unsayable, and when one finishes the chapter on "The Right Stuff" (21–43), one has what amounts to an extended definition of the term.

The book is not concerned with the mystery of the right stuff, its inexplicability, but precisely in explaining what makes those possessing that quality tick. It is not belittling *The Right Stuff* to say that it is minimally lyrical and presentational.

The similarities between *Rising from the Plains* and *The Right Stuff* are remarkable. Like McPhee, Wolfe uses a narrative structure to convey information about the Mercury project, the astronauts serving the same function as does David Love. The stretches of "pure" information are integral (unlike those in Irving Stone's *Passions of the Mind*), engaging the reader not as asides, but as central to the intention of the book.

In his first three chapters, Wolfe establishes his method and, in fact, prepares his readers for what is to come. The first chapter, "The Angels," begins thus:

> Within five minutes, or ten minutes, no more than that, three of the others had called her on the telephone to ask her if she had heard that something had happened out there.
> "Jane, this is Alice. Listen I just got a call from Betty, and she said she heard something's happened out there. Have you heard anything?" That was the way they phrased it, call after call. She picked up the telephone and began relaying this same message to some of the others.
> "Connie, this is Jane Conrad. Alice just called me, and she says something's happened. . . ."
> *Something* was part of the official Wife Lingo for tiptoeing blindfolded around the subject. (3)

And the subject, of course, was crashes of the pilots at Edwards who were attempting to show that they had *the right stuff*, and that is the subject of the first chapter.

The second chapter is an extended definition of "the right stuff," replete with statistics ("there was a 23 percent probability that he [a Navy pilot] would die in an aircraft accident" [22]), representative anecdotes ("But what about Ted Whelan, who fell like a rock from 8,100 feet when his parachute failed [35]?"), and explanations ("In fact, the feeling was so righteous, so exalted, it could become religious" [40]).

The third chapter, "Yeager," establishing the legendary Chuck Yeager as a foil character for the astronauts and, through the narrative concerning Yeager, giving the early history of supersonic flight, is a synecdoche for the whole book.

The chapter begins with a long representative anecdote about the archetypical airline pilot, who on his dawn approach to JFK announces, " 'Now, folks, uh . . . this is the captain . . . ummmm . . . We've got a little ol' red light up here on the control panel that's tryin' to tell us the *land*in' gears're not . . . uh . . . *lock*in' into position when we lower 'em . . . Now . . . I don't believe that little ol' red light knows what it's *talk*in' about' " (44). And so the captain, sounding almost bored, takes the plane down to 200 feet and flies past the tower, but the controllers can't tell whether the gear is locked in position or not, so the pilot tells the passengers he'll make a swing out over the ocean to dump some fuel, and the stewardesses show the passengers the correct position for a crash landing.

This "poker-hollow West Virginia drawl," imitated by pilots all over the nation, "was the drawl of the most righteous of all the possessors of the right stuff: Chuck Yeager" (46). A brief (two-page) biographical sketch of Yeager follows, and Wolfe, having established a character to give dramatic meaning to the information about supersonic flight, goes on to create the scene: "Muroc was up in the high elevations of the Mojave Desert. It looked like some fossil landscape that had long since been left behind by the rest of terrestrial evolution. It was full of huge dry lake beds, the biggest being Rogers Lake. Other than sagebrush the only vegetation was Joshua trees, twisted freaks of the plant world that looked like a cross between cactus and Japanese bonsai" (48). Now comes a canon, the themes of which are, first, the facts about supersonic flight and, second, the picture and spirit of Pancho's Fly Inn, social club of the Muroc pilots, presided over by Pancho Barnes, who was only forty-one, but "whose face was so weatherbeaten, had so many hard miles on it, that she looked older, especially to the young pilots at the base" (50).

The scene is set; the characters have been introduced; and we have learned that "The attempt to push beyond Mach 1—'breaking the sound barrier'—was set for October 14, 1947." End of Act I. Act II begins with a flashback to Sunday evening, October 12. Yeager and his wife Glennis have dropped into Pancho's to knock back a few, not because it was the weekend, but "because night had come and he was a pilot at Muroc" (53). At eleven o'clock or so, Yeager gets the idea that he and Glennis should go for ride on two of Pancho's horses, so they saddle up and gallop off into the moonlit desert. (In the movie, they took this ride in the daylight, but in this case, fidelity to history creates high drama, the vision of Chuck and Glennis racing among the Joshua trees through the silvery light and the shadows.)

The ride ends with Yeager running into a closed gate, being thrown, and breaking two ribs. "Yeager gets up before daybreak on Tuesday morning—which is supposed to be the day he tries to break the sound barrier—and his ribs still hurt like a sonofabitch. He gets his wife to drive him over to the field, and he has to keep his arm pinned down to his side to keep his ribs from hurting so much" (55). But having the right stuff and then some, Yeager does fly, even though he must smuggle a piece of broom handle aboard the X-1, in order to reach the door handle with his left arm.

Of course, Yeager did break the sound barrier on that Tuesday. The rest of the chapter tells of Yeager's career, of the "purity" of the Muroc base, and of its decline after America responded to Sputnik with the MISS Project—"Man in Space Soonest."

Some of the most righteous of the brethren weren't even eligible for the preliminary screening of Project Mercury. Yeager was young enough—still only thirty-five—but had never attended college. [Scott] Crossfield and Joe Walker were civilians. Not that any of them gave a damn . . . at the time. The commanding officer at Edwards passed the word around that he wanted his top boys, the test pilots in Fighter Ops, to avoid Project Mercury because it would be a ridiculous waste of talent; they would just become "Spam in a can." This phrase "Spam in a can" became very popular at Edwards as the nickname for Project Mercury. (78)

Wolfe's achievement in *The Right Stuff* is enormous. The book is the ideal example of its kind, a genre (including, of course, all of McPhee's works) that might be called "dramatic exposition." Wolfe's most recent work is a novel, *The Bonfire of the Vanities,* a revision of the serial version that he published in *Rolling Stone.* According to

Newsweek (Oct. 26, 1987), Wolfe intended the work to be a novel of the city, like those of Thackeray and Dickens, Balzac and Zola. However, the *Newsweek* judgment is accurate:

As one of Wolfe's New York cops would say, "Fuhgedaboudit." "The Bonfire of the Vanities" is a lot more fun than gritty realism—and a lot more in keeping with Wolfe's typographically adventuresome, high-spirited style. It's the Human Comedy, on a skyscraper scale and at a taxi-meter pace: an extravagantly hyperbolic send-up of The Way They Live Now—in the streets, the suites and the salons—of New York in the '80's. (Lehman 85)

The book is as lively as anything Wolfe has written, but in its value as literature, I think it falls well short of *The Right Stuff*. Its satire is too particular and local to have great staying power, and, paradoxically, the techniques of the literature of fact that Wolfe uses in his fiction do not work, as do the techniques of fiction that he uses in his literature of fact. For example, when he writes about the patrons of a Las Vegas casino, Wolfe has no way of determining their exact ages and thus guesses, but when he creates characters in fiction, he does know not only their exact ages, but everything else about them; hence, one questions descriptions such as the following: "He was about sixty, short, thin, bald, wiry, with a sharp nose, hollow eyes, and a grim set to his mouth" (*Bonfire* 41); "The driver was a swarthy fat man, pudgy, around fifty, or some gray-lard middle" (*Bonfire* 43).

The lambency of point of view in the novel destroys verisimilitude. We are experiencing a scene from the point of view of a character when suddenly the author *in propria persona* provides commentary that shatters the illusion. In one instance, Sherman McCoy, financial wizard of the bond market, is walking his dog in the rain along Park Avenue when he sees a black youth approaching.

Sherman stared at him. Well, let him come! I'm not budging! It's my territory! I'm not giving way for any street punks!

The black youth suddenly made a ninety degree turn and cut across the street to the sidewalk on the other side. The feeble yellow of a sodium-vapor streetlight reflected for an instant on his face as he checked Sherman out.

He had crossed over! What a stroke of luck!

Not once did it dawn on Sherman McCoy that what the boy had seen was a thirty-eight-year-old white man, soaking wet, dressed in some sort of military-looking raincoat full of straps and buckles, holding a violently lurching animal in his arms, staring, bug-eyed, talking to himself. (17)

The flat characters in *The Bonfire of the Vanities* serve the purposes of Wolfe's topical satire, but are uninteresting in themselves. (No Ahabs or Anna Kareninas here.) The "flat" characters in *The Right Stuff* are interesting, gaining their "roundness," first, from the reader's knowledge of the world to which the book refers and, second, from their informativeness.

In *The Atlantic* (December 1987), Nicholas Lemann criticized the novel for its ambivalence; the book, he said, wavered between satire and tragedy. Yet *"The Bonfire of the Vanities* is on the whole such a pleasure to read that the prospect of Wolfe's continued absence from journalism is actually bearable. But since his first novel is at heart an attempt at tragedy, it seems fair to hope that in the second one he'll try farce" (107).

It is terribly ungrateful to end the discussion of so versatile and satisfying a writer as Tom Wolfe with grumbling about his accomplishments; therefore, I will say that *The Bonfire of the Vanities* is less than satisfactory only in the context of the author's whole body of works; as a contemporary novel, the book ranks high in its readability and ingenuity. As Terrence Rafferty said in a *New Yorker* review, "It has everything that intelligent research, precision tooling, and strong, unambiguous opinions can give to a narrative, and almost nothing that the imagination, the urge to take oneself into unexplored areas, can" (91).

Hunter Thompson and the Literature of Self-Indulgence

In one of the earliest studies of the new journalism, Michael L. Johnson says that Hunter Thompson's style, in *Hell's Angels*, "is perfectly attuned to the subject matter, and Thompson keeps it true, modulating and adapting it throughout to different situations and different aspects of his reportage" (133). Johnson says of the book that it is thorough, documented, and fair—a classic piece of new journalism.

When the book appeared in 1966, it had the advantage of topicality; the Hell's Angels were news. Twenty years later, this in-depth study of an American subculture stands up very well and takes its place in literature with Margaret Mead's books on Samoa and New

Guinea, Frederick Lewis Allen's *Only Yesterday*, and Farley Mowat's *People of the Deer*, even with *The Oregon Trail* and *Two Years Before the Mast*. It is a book to be taken seriously.

Between *Hell's Angels* and *The Curse of Lono* (1983), Thompson by and large did two sorts of writing: "straight" journalism and "gonzo" journalism, a style of reporting, says Thompson in *The Great Shark Hunt*, based on William Faulkner's idea that the best fiction is far more *true* than any kind of journalism" (120) and needing

the talents of a master journalist, the eye of an artist/photographer and the heavy balls of an actor. Because the writer *must* be a participant in the scene, while he's writing it—or at least taping it, or even sketching it. Or all three. Probably the closest analogy to the ideal would be a film director/producer who writes his own scripts, does his own camera work and somehow manages to film himself in the action, as the protagonist or at least a main character. (120)

The main problem with gonzo journalism as practiced by Thompson is its singular uninformativeness: one learns a good deal about the author, very little about his subject. *Fear and Loathing on the Campaign Trail*, for instance, is an intense account of Thompson's prejudices, neuroses, and devotion to alcohol and drugs, but hardly either a portrait of the candidates (McGovern and Nixon) or an analysis of the issues.

On Edwin Muskie: "It was not until his campaign collapsed and his ex-staffers felt free to talk I learned working for Big Ed was something like being locked in a rolling boxcar with a vicious 200-pound water rat" (*Shark* 249).

On Hubert Humphrey: "Any political party that can't cough up anything better than a treacherous brain-damaged old vulture like Hubert Humphrey deserves every beating it gets. They don't hardly make 'em like Hubert any more—but just to be on the safe side, he should be castrated anyway" (*Shark* 250).

On George McGovern: "[H]e has crippled himself with a series of almost unbelievable blunders—Eagleton, Salinger, O'Brien, etc.—that have understandably convinced huge chunks of the electorate, including at least half of his own hard-core supporters, that the Candidate is a gibbering dingbat. His behavior since Miami has made a piecemeal mockery of everything he seemed to stand for during the primaries" (*Shark* 264).

The gonzo pieces dwell at length and lovingly on the stimulants and depressants that seem necessary for Thompson's functioning. For a session of writing in San Francisco, he was fortified, in his hotel room, by "two cases of Mexican beer, four quarts of gin, a dozen grapefruits, and enough speed to alter the outcome of six Super Bowls. There was also a big Selectric typewriter, two reams of paper, a face-cord of oak firewood and three tape recorders—in case the situation got so desperate that I might finally have to resort to verbal composition" (*Shark* 221).

And then there are the outrageous capers. Like the time he and Ralph Steadman attempted to paint "Fuck the Pope" on the side of an America's cup yacht (*Shark* 128–29) or his candidacy for the office of sheriff of Aspen, on a six-plank platform: (1) rip up all the asphalt streets and sod them; (2) change the name of Aspen to "Fat City"; (3) prosecute drug dealers who cheat their customers; (4) forbid hunting and fishing for all nonresidents; (5) disarm the sheriff and his deputies; (6) savagely harass anyone involved in land-rape (*Shark* 199–202).

Concurrently, however, Thompson was producing first-rate journalistic reports, such as an article on the Haight-Ashbury Hippies for the *New York Times Magazine* in 1967 (*Shark* 446–59) and a long piece on the death of Ruben Salazar, a Los Angeles newsman, published in *Rolling Stone* in 1971 (*Shark* 136–74).

In 1980, *Running* magazine asked Thompson to report on the Honolulu Marathon. Thompson accepted and asked his friend Ralph Steadman, an artist, to go along. As Thompson explains,

Journalism is a Ticket to Ride, to get personally involved in the same news other people watch on TV— which is nice, but it won't pay the rent, and people who can't pay their rent in the Eighties are going to be in trouble. . . .

Indeed. The time has come to write *books*—or even movies, for those who can keep a straight face. Because there is money in these things; and there is no money in journalism.

But there is *action*, and action is an easy thing to get hooked on. (*Curse* 57)

The *book* that Thompson writes, *The Curse of Lono*, is (1) a series of outrageous episodes in the mission, including frequent catalogues of the drugs and alcohol that the author et al. consumed; (2) arrestingly grotesque full-color and pen-and-ink illustrations by Ralph Steadman; (3) occasional interpolations, printed in blue boxes, from the sources that Thompson used in background "research" (e.g., Richard Hough, *The Last Voyage of Captain James Cook;* Mark Twain, *Letters from Hawaii;* and *The Journal of William Ellis*). After all, Thompson appears to be using exactly the same formula that served both John McPhee and Tom Wolfe so admirably: conveying information dramatically by embedding it in a narrative. However, in *The Curse of Lono,* as in the *Fear and Loathing* books, information is subordinated to the monomaniacal obsessions of the author; what emerges from the book is not knowledge about anything—the Honolulu Marathon, the history of Hawaii—except the compulsions and neuroses of the author. In one sense, the book is a confession, much like *The Armies of the Night,* but without that book's intelligence and compassion for others; in another sense, it is a pastiche of narrative and travelogue information, like *The Passions of the Mind.*

Here is the new journalism gone wild; as Ronald Weber has said of Thompson, he is a personal journalist with a vengeance (24).

What survived the disintegration of Thompson's gifts—or perhaps arose from their ashes—was the ability to portray a life without love, values, or interests. If one finds humor in his later work, as I sometimes do, it is black humor indeed, vitriolic, a sneer at the human condition. In fact, a little bit of *Fear and Loathing* or *The Curse of Lono* goes a long way.

Here is an example of Thompson at his mellowest:

> The British are very sentimental about Christmas. They want the snow and the slush of England, diseased beggars ringing bells on every street corner, news of food riots on the telly, the familiar sickening chill of a stone home with no furnace and the family huddled cheerfully around a pot of burning coal on Christmas morning. They are not comfortable with the idea of Saint Nick coming in on a surfboard with a sack full of cockroaches and a *TV Guide* filled with nothing but incomprehensible American "football" games for the next two weeks. (Lono 81)

At his outrageous worst, he is barely tolerable.

Follow the esthetic of the new journalism to its illogical conclusion, and one arrives at *The Curse of Lono.* In this sense, one can say that Hunter Thompson is the last of the new journalists.

CHAPTER 5
Form: The Essay

This book was written in good faith, reader. It warns you from the outset that in it I have set myself no goal but a domestic and private one. I have had no thought of serving either you or my own glory. My powers are inadequate for such a purpose. I have dedicated it to the private convenience of my relatives and friends, so that when they have lost me (as soon they must), they may recover here some features of my habits and temperament, and by this means keep the knowledge they have had of me more complete and alive.

If I had written to seek the world's favor, I should have bedecked myself better, and should present myself in a studied posture. I want to be seen here in my simple, natural, ordinary fashion, without straining or artifice; for it is myself that I portray. My defects will here be read to the life, and also my natural form, as far as respect for the public has allowed. Had I been placed among those nations which are said to live still in the sweet freedom of nature's first laws, I assure you I should very gladly have portrayed myself here entire and wholly naked.

Thus, reader, I am myself the matter of my book; you would be unreasonable to spend your leisure on so frivolous and vain a subject.

So farewell.

—Montaigne, "To the Reader"

To write just treatises requireth leisure in the writer, and leisure in the reader, and therefore are not so fit, neither in regard of your Highness' princely affairs, nor in regard of my continual services; which is the cause that hath made me choose to write certain brief notes, set down rather significantly than curiously, which I have called *Essays*. The word is late, but the thing is ancient. For Seneca's epistles to Lucilius, if one mark them well, are but *Essays*, that is, dispersed meditations, though conveyed in the form of epistles. These labours of mine I know cannot be worthy of your Highness, for what can be worthy of you? But my hope is, they may be grains of salt, that will rather give you an appetite than offend you with satiety.

—Francis Bacon, "To the Most High and Excellent Prince, Henry,
Prince of Wales, Duke of Cornwall, and Earl of Chester"

Montaigne and Bacon nicely sum up and, in their essays, illustrate the distinction between what has been called the *informal* essay (by such practitioners as Swift, Lamb, Hazlitt, DeQuincey, Mark Twain, Thurber, and E. B. White) and the *formal* essay (of, for instance, Addison, Johnson, Arnold, Mill, Newman, Pater, and Emerson). A set of truisms adequately characterizes these essay types in general: the informal essay is personal and not as highly structured as the formal; it is likely to be anecdotal; and the author has no obligation to assume a disinterested stance toward issues. The canonical essayists in the two schools are so well known that illustrations here would be superfluous.

In a learned and wise book, *A Theory of Discourse*, James L. Kinneavy makes distinctions that illuminate the nature and purposes of the essay. His model of the universe of discourse contains four galaxies: persuasive (e.g., advertising, political speeches), literary (e.g., short story, lyric poem), expressive (e.g., diaries, minority protests), and referential, the locus of the essay. The categories that make up referential discourse are scientific, informative, and exploratory.

Scientific discourse *proves* a point by arguing from accepted premises or by generalizing from particulars (i.e., through either deduction or induction). The "universal audience" (Perelman and Olbrechts-Tyteca 31–35) takes a point to be established if the premise seems tenable and the logic of the argument appears unflawed or if the evidence is compelling. Informative discourse does not "prove" anything, but merely provides "news," gives information. The audience accepts the information without proof if the source appears reliable.

For Kinneavy, exploratory discourse is the result and manifestation of cognitive dissonance, a condition of "wonder, instability, or discomfort" that comes about when observed facts clash with accepted premises or dogmas, precipitating the search for a new model of experience (102–3). For Montaigne, the essay was exploratory; as Zeiger points out, Montaigne "essayed" his ideas, examining them from various points of view, ready to abandon them if the *assay* (from the same French root as "essay") proved they were fool's gold (455).

Richard Selzer will be our exemplary exploratory essayist.

In characterizing what he calls "the expository essay," George Dillon might have been speaking about Francis Bacon's works, which represent the Western intellectual and cultural ideal much more nearly than do those of the Montaigne:

The expository essay as here understood has a rhetorical purpose beyond "conveying information": it attempts to convince the reader that its model of experience or the world is valid. It does not seek to engage the reader in a course of action, however, but rather in a process of reflection, and its means of convincing are accordingly limited to the use of evidence and logical proof and the posture of open-mindedness. These methods are also associated with the liberally educated person, who is meditative, reflective, clear-headed, unbiased, always seeking to understand experience freshly and to find things of interest in the world. (23)

Stephen Jay Gould will provide our example of this kind of expository essay.

In the present chapter, unsurprisingly, I want to shift standard terminology from "formal" and "informal" to "discursive" and "presentational." I will begin the peregrination with a discussion of a masterful discursive essay by Stephen Jay Gould; next I will turn to form in a group of presentational essays: Joan Didion's apposition, Lewis Thomas's sham enthymeme, organic form in Eiseley's work, and narrative as exploratory discourse in an essay by Richard Selzer.

A Discursive Essay by Stephen Jay Gould

The title is "Natural Selection and the Human Brain: Darwin *vs.* Wallace," and the first sentence is "In the south transept of Chartres cathedral, the most stunning of all medieval windows depicts the four evangelists as dwarfs sitting upon the shoulders of four Old Testament prophets—Isaiah, Jeremiah, Ezekiel, and Daniel." Gould then refers to Newton's aphorism—"if I have seen further, it is by standing on the shoulders of giants"—which leads him to mention a book on pre-Newtonian uses of the metaphor and Gould's explanation that the author, Columbia Sociologist of Science Robert K. Merton, "devoted much of his work to the study of multiple discoveries in science" (47), which is exactly what happened in the case of Darwin and Wallace.

One might ask why Gould would devote nearly a whole page of his essay to a lead-in when he might have begun directly by reminding the reader that Darwin and Wallace almost simultaneously developed theories of natural selection. The answer is obviously that Gould needed to establish his *ethical* argument by setting a tone and taking a stance. The first two paragraphs clearly remove the essay from a specialized field and place it in the cultural *commonplace*, which is the expository essay's natural habitat, its *agora*.

"Natural Selection and the Human Brain" is an example of Burke's *syllogistic progression*, "the form of a perfectly conducted argument, advancing step by step" (*Counter-Statement* 124).

The body of the essay is an explanation of the dialectic whereby Darwin and Wallace, up to a point, developed nearly identical theories of natural selection and of the way in which the theories diverged. In other words, the essay is essentially an analysis of scientific logic—but in terms of a human drama.

> Wallace has come down through history as Darwin's shadow. In public and private, Darwin was infallibly decent and generous to his younger colleague. He wrote to Wallace in 1870: "I hope it is a satisfaction to you to reflect—and very few things in my life have been more satisfactory to me—that we have never felt any jealousy toward each other, though in one sense rivals." Wallace, in return, was consistently deferential. In 1864, he wrote to Darwin: "As to the theory of Natural Selection itself, I shall always maintain it to be actually yours and yours only. You had worked it out in details I had never thought of, years before I had a ray of light on the subject, and my paper would never have convinced anybody or been noticed as more than an ingenious speculation, whereas your book has revolutionized the study of Natural History, and carried away captive the best men of the present age." (Gould, 48–49)

The gist of the disagreement between Wallace and Darwin hinges on the doctrine of strict selectionism, to which Wallace clung: all evolutionary developments must have been the result of adaptation for survival of the fittest. Darwin argued, however, (1) that adaptive change in one organ of a creature can lead to nonadaptive change in another organ and (2) that an organ developed for one function can perform another, nonselected function, as well. "In 1870, as he prepared *The Descent of Man*, Darwin wrote to Wallace: 'I grieve to differ from you, and it actually terrifies me and makes me constantly distrust myself. I fear we shall never quite understand each other' " (52).

The crisis came when Wallace attempted to understand the evolution of the human brain. He knew that the brains of savages were as large as those of civilized *men*. "Moreover, since cultural conditioning can integrate the rudest savage into our most courtly life, the rudeness itself must arise from a failure to use existing capacities, not from their absence: 'It is latent in the lower races, since under European training native military bands have been formed in many parts of the world, which have been able to perform creditably the best modern music' " (54). As Wallace said, "Natural selection could only have endowed savage man with a brain a few degrees superior to that of an ape, whereas he actually possesses one very little inferior to that of a philosopher" (55). The human brain must have been created by a Higher Power. Ironically, then, as Gould says, Wallace's hyperselectionism led directly back to the creationism that it was intended to replace.

Gould, very much like McPhee, has cast a technical discussion in the form of a drama, fashioning characters that will "humanize" the information: David Love, Alfred Russell Wallace, and Charles Darwin. These are quite different from the *composite characters* that Hollowell says are one of the devices of the new journalism (30). Nonetheless, the informativeness of the essay is its primary interest; the *technical* brilliance of the author in conveying that information engages only the specialized reader (such as a person who would write a book about the rhetoric of nonfiction), not the common reader. "Natural Selection and the Human Brain: Darwin *vs.* Wallace" contrasts starkly with the essays to be discussed hereafter.

Presentation: The Prose Lyric

From lyric poetry—not very popular nowadays, I think—we can learn much about attitudes, little about opinions; much about sense impressions, little about ideas. Such also is the case with many particularly satisfying "expository" essays that do not provide significant information or advance arguments, but, rather, dance attitudes.

Coherence: Apposition (Joan Didion)

The lyric in prose gains its coherence from what Burke called *qualitative progression,* in which "the presence of one quality prepares us for the introduction of another" (Burke, *Counter-Statement* 124), not from the syllogistic progression that structures "Natural Selection and the Human Brain."

In "Form, Authority, and the Critical Essay," Keith Fort serendipitously and convincingly explained what should have been, but was not, the obvious: available forms determine attitudes. If, for instance, the only form available to students for their responses to literature is the conventional expository essay, with its clear-cut topic and its tree-able structure, then the attitude expressed must affirm the discursiveness of literature. The prose lyric breaks out of the "syllogistic," linear, Western form and in so doing frees itself of the strictures of discursiveness.

The essential difference between the coherence of the discursive essay and that of the presentational essay can be expressed metaphorically. In its superstructure, the well formed discursive essay is a branching tree diagram or organizational chart with the topic, enthymeme, or macroproposition (van Dijk 42) at the top. In an image adapted from Kintsch ("Psychological Processes" 7–8), the form of a presentational essay is that of a galaxy, with dense clusters of bright stars related as subsystems within the whole as it spirals through the universe.

The prevailing dogma is that a clear-cut topic (in the scientistic language of van Dijk, a "macroproposition") is essential to coherence, but Witte and Faigley give a more useful view of coherence as "those underlying semantic relations that allow a text to be understood and used . . . conditions governed by the writer's purpose, the audience's knowledge and expectations, and the information to be conveyed" (202). In effect, *any text will be coherent if the reader takes it to be so*, and a case in point is *The Waste Land*, which Cleanth Brooks analyzed as a perfectly coherent whole (*Modern Poetry and the Tradition* 138–59) and Graham Hough likened to a painting with "pointillist technique in one part . . . and the glazes of the high renaissance in another" (*Reflections on a Literary Revolution* 38).

One of Wolfgang Iser's points—which will be discussed in some detail in the final chapter of this book—is that readers must fill "gaps" in the text and thus are actively involved in constructing, not merely recovering, the meaning. A passage quoted in Clark and Clark demonstrates that readers also construct global representations (i.e., coherent wholes) from the individual sentences of a text:

The two of them glanced nervously at each other as they approached the man standing there expectantly. He talked to them for about ten minutes, but spoke loudly enough that everyone else in the room could hear too. Eventually he handed over two objects he had been given, one to each of them. After he had said a few more words, the ordeal was over. With her veil lifted, the two of them kissed, turned around, and rushed from the room arm in arm, with everyone else falling in behind. (161)

Readers eventually realize that the scene is a wedding, even though no individual sentence in the passage says as much, and the text becomes a coherent whole.

Clark and Clark also quote a story from a study by Bransford and Johnson. One group of readers was given the title *Watching a Peace March from the Fortieth Floor* and another group the title *A Space Trip to an Inhabited Planet*. Because of one sentence in the passage—"The landing was gentle and luckily the atmosphere was such that no special suits had to be worn"—the readers of *A Space Trip to an Inhabited Planet* found the passage much more coherent than did the readers of the other title:

The view was breathtaking. From the window one could see the crowd below. Everything looked extremely small from such a distance, but the colorful costumes could still be seen. Everyone seemed to be moving in one direction in an orderly fashion and there seemed to be little children as well as adults. The landing was gentle and luckily the atmosphere was such that no special suits had to be worn. At first there was a great deal of activity. Later, when the speeches started, the crowd quieted down. The man with the television camera took many shots of the setting and the crowd. Everyone was very friendly and seemed glad when the music started. (163)

The point is, of course, that the problematic sentence fits readers' (sci-fi) world knowledge about space travel and conflicts with views from the fortieth floor.

Joan Didion's "Los Angeles Notebook" is a series of five sketches in eight pages, adding up to an ideal example of qualitative progression in a prose lyric: an attitudinal characterization of Los Angeles. The subjects of the sketches are:
(1) The Santa Ana wind:

The Pacific turned ominously glossy during a Santa Ana period, and one woke in the night troubled not only by the peacocks screaming in the olive trees but by the eerie absence of surf. (217–18)

(2) A late-night radio talk show:

So it went, from midnight until 5 a.m., interrupted by records and by occasional calls debating whether or not a rattlesnake can swim. Misinformation about rattlesnakes is a leitmotif of the insomniac imagination in Los Angeles. (221)

(3) Wearing a bikini to a supermarket on a hot, smoggy Sunday afternoon:

That is not a very good thing to wear to the market but neither is it, at Ralph's on the corner of Sunset and Fuller, an unusual costume. Nonetheless a large woman in a cotton muumuu jams her cart into mine at the butcher counter. "*What a thing to wear to the market*," she says in a loud but strangled voice. (222–23)

(4) The bored sophistication of movie people:

A party at someone's house in Beverly Hills: a pink tent, two orchestras, a couple of French Communist directors in Cardin evening jackets, chili and hamburgers from Chasen's. (223)

(5) Piano bars:

A drunk requests "The Sweetheart of Sigma Chi." The piano player doesn't know it. "Where'd you learn to play the piano?" the drunk asks. "I got two degrees," the piano player says. "One in musical education." (224)

Through what Chris Anderson calls her "radical particularity" (4), Didion creates an attitudinally coherent essay. "Her habitual gesture as a stylist is to isolate the ironic or symbolic or evocative image and then reflect on its possible significance" (Anderson 134). "Los Angeles Notebook" is a series of these images in *apposition*.

In "Brain, Rhetoric, and Style," I characterized what I then called the "appositional" essay as follows:

1. The topic is implied, not stated directly. (I would now say that the reader may derive or create a topic or macroproposition.)
2. As opposed to the rigid organization of what I called the "propositional" (i.e., "discursive"), appositional organization is flexible (i.e., appositional).
3. Examples are specific (as in the "radical particularity" of Joan Didion).
4. As opposed to the backgrounded style of the propositional essay, the appositional style is foregrounded. To use the foregrounded style is "to present phenomena in a fully externalized form, visible and palpable in all their parts, and completely fixed in spatial and temporal relations" (Auerbach 6).
5. Finally, the appositional essay has great presence. (135–36)

In fact, these characteristics are a pretty good description of an essay such as "Los Angeles Notebook."

Coherence: The Sham Enthymeme (Lewis Thomas)

If asked to state the thesis of the title essay in Lewis Thomas's collection *Late Night Thoughts on Listening to Mahler's Ninth Symphony*, the common reader, attempting to explain the nearly unsayable lyric experience in discursive terms, would probably say something like this: "The realization that humankind can annihilate itself is depressing." But this is much like boiling "To His Coy Mistress" down to the aphorism *carpe diem* and demeans the experience that the essay provides—as a colleague of mine once said, selling your soul for a pot of message.

"Late Night Thoughts on Listening to Mahler's Ninth Symphony" is short enough to be included here in its entirety.

1. I cannot listen to Mahler's Ninth Symphony with anything like the old melancholy mixed with the high pleasure I used to take from this music. There was a time, not long ago, when what I heard, especially in the final movement, was an open acknowledgment of death and at the same time a quiet celebration of the tranquility connected to the process. I took this music as a metaphor for reassurance, confirming my own strong hunch that the dying of every living creature, the most natural of all experiences, has to be a peaceful experience. I rely on nature. The long passages on all the strings at the end, as close as music can come to expressing silence itself, I used to hear as Mahler's idea of leave-taking at its best. But always, I have heard this music as a solitary, private listener, thinking about death.

2. Now I hear it differently. I cannot listen to the last movement of the Mahler Ninth without the doorsmashing intrusion of a huge new thought: death everywhere, the dying of everything, the end of humanity. The easy sadness expressed with such gentleness and delicacy by that repeated phrase on faded strings, over and over again, no longer comes to me as old, familiar news of the cycle of living and dying. All through the last notes my mind swarms with images of a world in which the thermonuclear bombs have begun to explode, in New York and San Francisco, in Moscow and Leningrad, in Paris, in Paris, in Paris. In Oxford and Cambridge, in Edinburgh. I cannot push away the thought of a cloud of radioactivity drifting along the Engadin [*sic*], from the Moloja Pass to Ftan, killing off the part of the earth I love more than any other part.

3. I am old enough by this time to be used to the notion of dying, saddened by the glimpse when it has occurred but only transiently knocked down, able to regain my feet quickly at the thought of continuity, any day.

I have acquired and held in affection until very recently another sideline of an idea which serves me well at dark times: the life of the earth is the same as the life of an organism: the great round being possesses a mind: the mind contains an infinite number of thoughts and memories: when I reach my time I may find myself still hanging around in some sort of midair, one of those small thoughts, drawn back into the memory of the earth: in that particular sense I will be alive.

4. Now all that has changed. I cannot think that way anymore [sic]. Not while those things are still in place, aimed everywhere, ready for launching.

5. This is a bad enough thing for the people in my generation. We can put up with it, I suppose, since we must. We are moving along anyway, like it or not. I can even set aside my private fancy about hanging around, in midair.

6. What I cannot imagine, what I cannot put up with, the thought that keeps grinding its way into my mind, making the Mahler into a hideous noise close to killing me, is what it would be like to be young. How do the young stand it? How can they keep their sanity? If I were very young, sixteen or seventeen years old, I think I would begin, perhaps very slowly and imperceptibly, to go crazy.

7. There is a short passage near the very end of the Mahler in which the almost vanishing violins, all engaged in a sustained backward glance, are edged aside for a few bars by the cellos. Those lower notes pick up fragments from the first movement, as though prepared to begin everything all over again, and then the cellos subside and disappear, like an exhalation. I used to hear this as a wonderful few seconds of encouragement: we'll be back, we're still here, keep going, keep going.

8. Now, with a pamphlet in front of me on a corner of my desk, published by the Congressional Office of Technology Assessment, entitled *MX Basing*, an analysis of all the alternative strategies for placement and protection of hundreds of these missiles, each capable of creating artificial suns to vaporize a hundred Hiroshimas, collectively capable of destroying the life of any continent, I cannot hear the same Mahler. Now, those cellos sound in my mind like the opening of all the hatches and the instant before ignition.

9. If I were sixteen or seventeen years old, I would not feel the cracking of my own brain, but I would know for sure that the whole world was coming unhinged. I can remember with some clarity what it was like to be sixteen. I had discovered the Brahms symphonies. I knew that there was something going on in the late Beethoven quartets that I would have to figure out, and I knew that there was plenty of time ahead for all the figuring I would ever have to do. I had never heard of Mahler. I was in no hurry. I was a college sophomore and had decided that Wallace Stevens and I possessed a comprehensive understanding of everything needed for life. The years stretched away forever ahead, forever. My great-great

grandfather had come from Wales, leaving his signature in the family Bible on the same page that carried, a century later, my father's signature. It never crossed my mind to wonder about the twenty-first century; it was just there, given, somewhere in the sure distance.

10. The man on television, Sunday midday, middle-aged and solid, nice-looking chap, all the facts at his fingertips, more dependable looking than most high-school principals, is talking about civilian defense, his responsibility in Washington. It can make an enormous difference, he is saying. Instead of the outright death of eighty million American citizens in twenty minutes, he says, we can, by careful planning and practice, get that number down to only forty million, maybe even twenty. The thing to do, he says, is to evacuate the cities quickly and have everyone get under shelter in the countryside. That way we can recover, and meanwhile we will have retaliated, incinerating all of Soviet society, he says. What about radioactive fallout? he is asked. Well, he says. Anyway, he says, if the Russians know they can only destroy forty million of us instead of eighty million, this will deter them. Of course, he adds, they have the capacity to kill all two hundred and twenty million of us if they were to try real hard, but they know we can do the same to them. If the figure is only forty million this will deter them, not worth the trouble, not worth the risk. Eighty million would be another matter, we should guard ourselves against losing that many all at once, he says.

11. If I were sixteen or seventeen years old and had to listen to that, or read things like that, I would want to give up listening and reading. I would begin thinking up new kinds of sounds, different from any music heard before, and I would be twisting and turning to rid myself of human language.

In this lyric, only the unsayable, the presentational, makes sense; the discursive, the expository, is madness.

The very title evokes the swelling lament of the symphony's first movement, but Thomas is preoccupied with the final movement, the adagio: an indeterminate text which once had been "a metaphor for reassurance, confirming my own strong hunch that the dying of every living creature, the most natural of all experiences, has to be a peaceful experience." But now the meaning has changed. From the call of the horns and the inconstancy of the strings fading almost into silence and then surging back, Thomas derives a meaning that, in the second paragraph, he conveys through a panoramic image of worldwide thermonuclear devastation, concluding specifically with the area that he loves more than any other part of earth, the Engadine.

The third paragraph begins prosaically enough with a statement about Thomas's reconciliation to the idea of death, but then modulates from statement to another image: that luminous blue and white ball, the earth as seen from outer space, "the great round being," as an organism, with a mind of which Thomas would be a small part after his death.

What has transformed the meaning of the Ninth into "a hideous noise" is the thought of the young, who could, like Thomas, have discovered Wallace Stevens, Brahms, and Beethoven; who, from the records of their forebears, could have derived assurance of the future; but who must now live with the *facts* of the thermonuclear age. The melody near the end of the Ninth no longer says, "We'll be back, we're still here, keep going, keep going" because a freakish intertextuality—the discursive facts of a pamphlet on *MX Basing* and a television talk on civil defense by a government official—has changed the symphony's conclusion into the unintelligible cacophony of silo hatches opening.

Thomas has gone as far as language will carry him, but that isn't far enough. To "say" what needs to be said, young people would need to invent a new kind of music, for the old kind is inadequate, and human language, with its rational statement of the facts, is merely a curse to be exorcised, an unbearable torment.

Unlike "Los Angeles Notebook," "Late Night Thoughts" does have an easily derivable enthymeme or macroproposition, stated earlier (somewhat invidiously, to be sure) as "The realization that humankind can annihilate itself is depressing," but paradoxically, the real message is that the real "message" is unsayable, even unthinkable—beyond comprehension and hence beyond expression. One might say, then, that Thomas's enthymeme is a sham.

A tree diagram of "Los Angles Notebook" is one-dimensional, as shown in Figure 5–1.

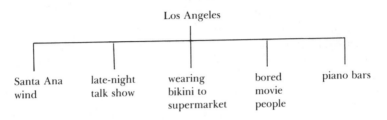

Figure 5-1. The structure of "Los Angeles Notebook," by Joan Didion.

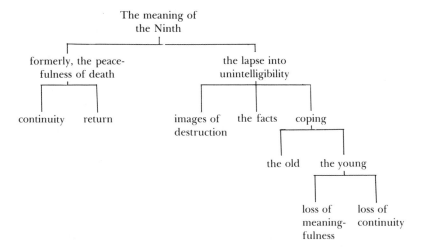

Figure 5-2. The structure of "Late Night Thoughts on Listening to Mahler's Ninth Symphony," by Lewis Thomas.

A tree of "Late Night Thoughts," as in Figure 5–2, is a superstructure that could well be that of a discursive essay.

But neither "Los Angeles Notebook" nor "Late Night Thoughts" advances an argument, as does "Darwin vs. Wallace"; neither is informative in the sense of reducing the reader's uncertainty about a topic or of supplying fresh data; nonetheless, both are, in my opinion at least, particularly satisfying and convincing.

Organic Form in Loren Eiseley's Essays

Leafing through the works of Loren Eiseley, one finds, on page after page, brilliant metaphors, such as this one from the first page of *The Unexpected Universe:* "Every man contains within himself a ghost continent—a place circled as warily as Antarctica was circled two hundred years ago by Captain James Cook," or this one from the first page of *The Immense Journey:* "Some lands are flat and grass-covered, and smile so evenly up at the sun that they seem forever youthful, untouched by man or time. Some are torn, ravaged and convulsed like the features of profane old age." And throughout the essays, one finds anecdotes from which the teller draws lessons. One of the most dramatic, though too long to quote in its entirety, is the beginning of "The Angry Winter":

I had been huddled beside the fire one winter night, with the wind prowling outside and shaking the windows. The big shepherd dog on the hearth before me occasionally glanced up affectionately, sighed, and slept. I was working, actually, admidst the debris of a far greater winter. On my desk lay the lance points of ice age hunters and the heavy leg bone of a fossil bison. No remnants of flesh attached to these relics. The deed lay more than ten thousand years remote. It was represented here by naked flint and by bone so mineralized it rang when struck. As I worked on in my little circle of light, I absently laid the bone beside me on the floor. The hour had crept toward midnight. A grating noise, a heavy rasping of big teeth diverted me. I looked down.

The dog had risen. That rock-hard fragment of vanished beast was in his jaws and he was mouthing it with a fierce intensity I had never seen exhibited by him before.

"Wolf," I exclaimed, and stretched out my hand. The dog backed up but did not yield. A low and steady rumbling began to rise in his chest, something out of a long-gone midnight. There was nothing in that bone to taste, but ancient shapes were moving in his mind and determining his utterance. Only fools gave up bones. He was warning me. (93–94)

There follows an essay, concerning evolution and ecology, among other topics, which ends with another anecdote. When he was a young man, Eiseley set out for a long walk on a "sullen November day," finally, at twilight, reaching the town cemetery. There among the dead, he finds life: a jackrabbit.

We both had a fatal power to multiply, the thought flashed on me, and the planet was not large. Why was it so, and what was the message that somehow seemed spoken from a long way off beyond an ice field, out of all possible human hearing?

The snow lifted and swirled about us once more. He was going to need that broken bit of shelter [provided by a slab]. The temperature was falling. For his frightened, trembling body in all the million years between us, there had been no sorcerer's aid. He had survived alone in the blue nights and the howling dark. He was thin and crumpled and small.

Step by step I drew back among the dead and their fallen stones. Somewhere, if I could follow the fence lines, there would be a fire for me. For a moment I could see his ears nervously recording my movements, but I was a wraith now, fading in the storm.

"There are so few tracks in all this snow," someone had once protested. It was true. I stood in the falling flakes and pondered it. Even my own tracks were filling. But out of such desolation had arisen man, the desolate. In essence, he is a belated phantom of the angry winter. He carried, and perhaps will always carry, its cruelty and its springtime in his heart. (119)

It would appear that Eiseley the essayist is a practicing Romantic, following the leads of his anecdotes and metaphors, not aiming them—as does Gould, for instance—toward a clear-cut semantic intention.

As a long-time admirer of Eiseley's work, one who has with great pleasure been reading and rereading the essays for twenty years, I can say without intending criticism that the essays are structurally a-logical, but not quite, either, examples of qualitative progression. They gain their structure through the "perspective by incongruity" that results when Eiseley follows the implications of his "representative anecdotes."

In chapter two of this book, the nature and function of representative anecdotes was discussed, but we need to ponder Burke's "perspective by incongruity," which is "A method for gauging situations by verbal 'atom cracking.' That is, a word belongs by custom to a certain category—and by rational planning you wrench it loose and metaphorically apply it to a different category" (*Attitudes Toward History* 308). Then, of course, you follow the particles set free in the "cracking." The result is a "*dramatic* vocabulary, with weighting and counter-weighting, in contrast with the liberal ideal of *neutral* naming in the characterization of processes" (*Attitudes* 311).

Structurally, "The Hidden Teacher" is a series of anecdotes:

1. A retelling of the Job story. "A youth standing by, one Elihu, also played a role in this drama, for he ventured diffidently to his protesting elder that it was not true that God failed to manifest Himself. He may speak in one way or another, though men do not perceive it" (48–49).
2. The anecdote of the spider, which will be discussed in a moment.
3. The anecdote of the seed. "Its flexible limbs were stiffer than milkweed down, and, propelled by the wind, it ran rapidly and evasively over the pavement. It was like a gnome scampering somewhere with a hidden packet—for all I could tell, a totally new one: one of the jumbled alphabets of life" (56–57).
4. The anecdote of the mathematical genius, demonstrating his prowess to school children. "Like some heavy-browed child at the wood's edge, clutching the last stone hand ax, I was witnessing the birth of a new type of humanity—one so beyond its teachers that it was being used for mean purposes while the intangible web of the

universe in all its shimmering mathematical perfection glistened untaught in the mind of a chance little boy" (58).

5.   The anecdote of the archaeologist at Palenque. "After shining his torch over hieroglyphs and sculptured figures, the explorer remarked wonderingly: 'We were the first people for more than a thousand years to look at it' " (60).

6.   The anecdote of the young linguistics student who ultimately became Eiseley's revered professor. "The young student published a paper upon Mohegan linguistics, the first of a long series of studies upon the forgotten languages and ethnology of the Indians of the Northeastern forests. He had changed his vocation and turned to anthropology because of the attraction of a hidden teacher. But just who was the teacher? The young man himself, his instructor, or that solitary speaker of a dying tongue who had so yearned to hear her people's voice that she had softly babbled it to a child?" (62–63).

7.   The anecdote of the dream, in which a writer sees his dead father and mother through a window and then realizes that he is looking only at his own reflection. "My line was dying, but I understood. I hope they understood, too" (66).

The anecdote of the spider is a synecdoche for the structure of Eiseley's essays.

I once received an unexpected lesson from a spider.

It happened far away on a rainy morning in the West. I had come up a long gulch looking for fossils, and there, just at eye level, lurked a huge yellow-and-black orb spider, whose web was moored to the tall spears of buffalo grass at the edge of the arroyo. It was her universe, and her senses did not extend beyond the lines and spokes of the great wheel she inhabited. Her extended claws could feel every vibration throughout that delicate structure. She knew the tug of wind, the fall of a raindrop, the flutter of a trapped moth's wing. Down one spoke of the web ran a stout ribbon of gossamer on which she could hurry out to investigate her prey.

Curious, I took a pencil from my pocket and touched a strand of the web. Immediately there was a response. The web, plucked by its menacing occupant, began to vibrate until it was a blur. Anything that had brushed claw or wing against that amazing snare would be thoroughly entrapped. As the vibrations slowed, I could see the owner fingering her guidelines for signs of struggle. A pencil point was an intrusion into this universe for which no precedent existed. Spider was circumscribed by spider ideas; its universe was spider universe. All outside was irrational, extraneous, at best, raw material for spider. As I proceeded my way along the gully, like a vast

impossible shadow, I realized that in the world of spider I did not exist.
(49–50)

Stripped of its context, the lesson that Eiseley learned from the
spider is nugatory: the realization that "among the many universes
in which the world of living creatures existed, some were large,
some small, but all, including man's, were in some way limited or
finite" (51); however, the anecdote validates the lesson, just as a
fable validates the moral or as a lyric poem validates whatever
enthymeme can be derived from it.

In any case, Eiseley tells us that many times he has pondered his
encounter with the orb spider, and that "a message has arisen only
now from the misty shreds of that webbed universe" (51). The
message, though, turns out to be a question that leads to a *non
sequitur:*

Was it that spidery indifference to the human triumph?
If so, that triumph was very real and could not be denied. (51)

Paraphrased, these sentences are saying, "If the message was that
spidery indifference to the human triumph, that triumph was very
real and could not be denied," and this simply does not compute.
However, the lapse in *syllogistic progression* hardly matters, for the
reader is following the implications of the anecdotes, which are
heuristic.

What is the triumph? One cannot, as a matter of fact, be certain.
It is either the emergence of the human species or the scientific
achievement of tracing that emergence.

I saw, had seen many times, both mentally and in the seams of exposed
strata, the long backward stretch of time whose recovery is one of the great
feats of modern science. I saw the drifting cells of the early seas from which
all life, including our own, has arisen. The salt of those ancient seas is in
our blood, its lime is in our bones. Every time we walk along a beach some
ancient urge disturbs us so that we find ourselves shedding shoes and
garments, or scavenging among seaweed and whitened timbers like the
homesick refugees of a long war. (51)

The "refugees of war" metaphor opens a new pathway for Eiseley
to follow: "And war it has been indeed—the long war of life against
its inhospitable environment, a war that has lasted for perhaps three

billion years" (51): from the first seething of chemicals in a world without oxygen through the age of the ferns to the human brain, "so frail, so perishable, so full of inexhaustible dreams and hungers" (52).

To fault the essays because their author follows leads other than the logical is to miss the whole point of these prose lyrics, which advance by what might be called *anecdotal progression*.

Narrative as Exploratory Discourse in an Essay by Richard Selzer

Eiseley's "anecdotal progression" contrasts with the structure of a typical essay by Richard Selzer, who often builds on the scaffolding of one autobiographical narrative. One might call the structure of an essay such as "Diary of an Infidel: Notes from a Monastery" narrative progression.

The first essay in *Taking the World in for Repairs* (1986), this piece, somewhat of an anomaly because of its sixty- seven-page length, is an account of Selzer's spiritual struggle while he stayed (for an indefinite period, but apparently several weeks) in the monastery of San Giorgio Maggiore on an island in the Bay of Venice. The agon is that of an infidel physician trying to comprehend the faith of Benedictine monks, even tentatively, warily, attempting to gain a faith of his own.

In discussing this wonderful piece, it is unlikely that I will be able to shed new light on the nature of narrative *per se;* my more modest goal will be to analyze the use of narrative for referential (e.g., scientific, exploratory, explanatory) purposes and to express my appreciation for Richard Selzer's work.

One point worth repeating is the notion that coherence results when a reader is able to derive a "macroproposition" from a text and to understand how subordinate propositions relate to it and to one another in a structure that can be represented by a tree diagram (van Dijk; Kintsch). Yet any reader of stories understands that wrenching (or wringing) an enthymeme from *The Ambassadors* or *Women in Love* simply distorts the *real* nature of the *real* reader's response.

In the second chapter of this book, I explained Northrop Frye's account of how the reader constructs a plotted poetic work: after the reading, Frye says, the incidents regroup themselves around a theme ("Myth" 23). If *The Bonfire of the Vanities*, for example, is what

I take it to be, namely, a fictional narrative, and if the theme is what I take it to be, namely, the volatile values of upper-class New York (or of American society in general), then I begin to organize the work according to a series of categories—wealth, profession, appurtenances (residence, auto, furnishings, clothes), perks (reception in a restaurant by the headwaiter)—each of which derives from scenes in the book. From the narrative, I learn what it is to *experience* these values. No small lesson.

However, if I take *Bonfire* to be reference discourse, I will derive from it an organizational pivot, an enthymeme that I can argue pro or con and, in principle, prove or disprove—for example, "Based as they are on the material symbols of success, Yuppie values are shallow and corrupt."

Of course, I have taken "Diary of an Infidel" to be an essay—even though the front flap of the dust jacket of my copy says, "*Taking the World in for Repairs* consists of a dozen stories, essays and memoirs pertinent to the life of a doctor. . . . Each piece is a blend of fact and fiction." What, then, is "Diary of an Infidel"? Is it more akin to an autobiographical fiction such as *Look Homeward Angel*, to a first-person nonfiction narrative such as *Friendly Fire*, to a discursive essay such as "Darwin *vs.* Wallace," or to a presentational essay like "Late Night Thoughts"?

The answer to that question depends on what the reader expects to get from the narrative, i.e., the sort of speech act the reader takes the essay to be: a plotted poetic work (Frye, "Myth") or reference discourse (Kinneavy 73–210)? (Needless to say, on one reading "Diary" can be poetic and on another referential, but as Foley [25–41] has explained, it cannot be both at the same time.) Obviously, a narrative text can have a "scientific" or "explanatory" purpose (e.g, Dian Fossey's *Gorillas in the Mist;* Alan Moorehead's *Gallipoli*). Richard Selzer's "Diary of an Infidel" can be taken as exploratory discourse.

"Diary" has all of the features of a good autobiography or work of fiction: roundedness in characters; fully developed scenes; and conflict. More important, the argument of the essay arises from the drama and is part of it. In other texts, the drama only serves the purposes of the argument.

The narrative begins with the author (or his persona) unable to find a room in Venice. He sights the Abbey of San Giorgio Maggiore and, knowing the rule that the monks will provide a bed and food since "the most unlikely visitor has the possibility of having Christ within him" (13), takes a *vaporetto* to the island on which the abbey is situated, but informs the reader, "Long ago I accepted the notion that faith is something given to selected men and women, like perfect pitch. It cannot be sought after" (14).

The guestmaster, Dom Pietro, greets Selzer and takes him to his room, saying, "Enter, Christ," to which Selzer replies, "Well, not exactly" (15).

The next nine pages recount the guest's first night in the abbey, establishing his attitude and creating the scene. He hears the monks chant their vespers, meets the Abbott and kisses his ring, and at supper is unable to finish the soup or the "hard gray meat encased in a jelly" (18), which occasions the first conflict between the infidel and his hosts.

The abbot tells Selzer, "It is the rule here that you must finish everything on your plate" (18).

"Then permit me to serve myself."
"It is my pleasure to serve my guests."
"But you all eat so much. One is not accustomed."
"Saint Benedict has said that he who works shall eat."
"Then I must have work to do here. You must give me a job. I am not comfortable when I am idle and all about me are fully engaged."
"There is no work for you here."
"Then I am to be an ornament? Please, I am a doctor; I can give the monks each a physical examination. Or, if you prefer, I would be happy to help in the kitchen or laundry. The garden. Whatever."
"No," he smiles. "You are not to work here."
"But I have always worked. Upon my tombstone shall be carved 'He kept busy.' "
"No."
"Then why am I here?"
"The reason has not yet been revealed to me." The small white hands part briefly, then rejoin, and I understand that the subject is closed. (18–19)

The irony of the question "Then why am I here?" and the answer given by the abbot are revealed, as we shall see, only toward the end of the essay, but clearly both Selzer and the abbot believe that there is a higher cause than the need for food and shelter. Changing the subject with an apparently irrelevant (but fortuitous) question, the abbot asks, "Is there an English word—*tempiternal?* I read it the other day. How does it differ from *sempiternal?*" " 'I think it was a misprint,' I tell him" (19).

Alone in his room at last, Selzer feels a sense of homecoming, as if he had lived there before, and even the *Orario Monastico* listing the morrow's activities "seems no different from my own hectic hours in surgery where bits and pieces of day and night are pinched off, each full of its own obligation and necessity, though unannounced by bells" (24).

The first eleven pages begin to explore the relationship between the worldly and the spiritual and arrive at the tentative conclusion that the two are not mutually incompatible.

On the first morning, the abbot gives Selzer a tour of the monastery. The Palladian church—without the usual stained glass that Selzer resents—is "a vaulting paradise where voices ascend, multiply and are gathered beneath the dome, where pillars and arches stretch away and away in every direction into far distant darkness" (25). In the Conclave Room, Selzer seats himself unknowingly "in the place of the man who was elected pope in this room" (26) and horrifies the abbot and the other monks.

Now Selzer begins to develop one of the main characters, Dom Pietro:

His voice is baritone with just the hint of brogue. He is, after all, Irish from Dublin. The eyes are Anglo-Saxon blue; the nose fleshy with mobile nostrils. When he turns to speak, it is with his whole body rather than his head only, as though he were on stage playing to an audience. It is a flattering gesture in that it lends the impression that his entire attention is given to you alone. Turning, he lightly fingers the material of the habit which he does not so much wear as model. (27)

The Dom Pietro section goes on for about three pages (27–30), at the end of which the guestmaster is established as an interesting person in his own right, regardless of what Frye would call his allegorical value, whereby he represents a quality, idea, or philosophy ("Myth, Fiction, and Displacement" 23–24).

Pietro explains that the discipline and uniformity of their life "sets the stage for the appearance of God" (Selzer 28). But each time he leaves Selzer's room, Selzer turns the crucifix away from himself thirty degrees, to get out of the direct line of fire, and Pietro realigns it when he comes in again.

On an excursion to the city with Selzer, Pietro wolfs down two "heavy moist sweet cakes," plus half of Selzer's. Pietro, then, in his vanity and gluttony, has a worldly side just as surely as Selzer has spiritual longings.

This section ends with a visit to a convent. From behind a wooden lattice, the abbess visits with Selzer and Pietro as they drink wine. Selzer asks the abbess how long she has been in the convent. Twenty years.

"What do you do all day?"
"We pray. At night too. We are busy all the time and very happy." It is apparent that she has foretold my doubt. Pietro and the abbess engage in a long informal chat in Italian during which they both bubble over with what can only be construed as unalloyed pleasure. It is the shared experience of prayer that binds them together. Once again I am a goy among the Jews. (30)

Pietro, the holy man with worldly appetites, is established as the foil of Selzer, the worldly man with spiritual longings. Obviously it is difficult, if not impossible, to be "pure" in any sense.

Now, through a dramatic vignette, the theme changes, to the nature of love. In the refectory, the abbot, becoming annoyed at two of the older monks who are rather noisily enjoying a joke, abashes and deflates them by commanding, "*Piano!Piano!*"

"Do you love each other?" I ask the abbot.
"Oh yes. We do. They are brothers. I am their father. Of course I love them. But they must be ruled, like all children." He laughs genteelly. I see that he does love them, but not the way my father loved me nor the way I love my children. He loves them the way a shepherd loves his flock, or a mariner his crew, without passion and without recklessness but with an undercurrent of mistrust. The abbot sees my embarrassment for the monks. (34)

A bit later, Selzer encounters Vittorio, the novice master, kneeling before the altar in the Conclave Room, in a trance of prayer and devotion. "Has he eaten some marvelous drug? Hashish? Mushrooms?" (36).

Selzer realizes "There is no speck of egotism in his [Vittorio's] love, while the love I have known has been full of nothing else"— which brings the author to feel "for the first time the painful absence of God" (36). He is beginning to understand a spectrum of love that he had never known and finds even that "the coast of Venice seems farther away, receding" (41) as he becomes more and more a part of the monastery.

The last part of the essay—more than half of it—tells of the retreat from the monastery and back into the world, a peripety that comes about when Selzer arrives at his critique of spiritual love: "Along with human love, what is missing here is reproduction. Nothing, no one is born here. There are no new eyes, new breaths. There are no natives; everyone has come from somewhere else. All the fecundity is in the long ago. It stopped at the womb of Mary" (43).

The highest level generality—the "topic," the "macroproposition," the "enthymeme"—comes thirty pages before the end of the essay. It is the conclusion that Selzer has drawn from *exploring* his experiences: "To search for faith in a monastery is to deny its existence elsewhere. True morality is directed outward toward others. It has nothing to do with self- perfection. Besides it is less what goes into a man than what comes out of him that matters" (49).

A series of examples support his thesis. Adele Cleary worked in a postoperative recovery room for thirty-five years, caring for patients who would never know that she had been present. When she retired,

The chief of surgery proposed a toast with ginger ale.
"What are you going to do now, Adele?" he asked.
"Now?" said Adele with a shy smile. "Now I am going to recover from my life." (48)

And there was Wayne Flye, the self-effacing young surgeon who allowed Selzer to understand "a faithfulness to vocation, a testimony to the exorbitant demands of two hearts—the patient's, heaving there within view, and his own" (50–51).

More important, Selzer finds his own vocation again, as a physician, diagnosing and treating a monk afflicted with hyperthyroidism and, in a triumph of sorts, lancing a huge, painful carbuncle between the abbot's shoulder blades.

The story has been told. The argument is completed. Selzer leaves the monastery, crossing the water on a *vaporetto*. An unforgettable concluding image sums up "The Diary of an Infidel" and also, in a way, the *Leitmotif* of this chapter:

All at once, the sun sinks behind Venice and, as it does, for one precise moment the final rays strike the facade of the monastery, turning it red. Every window is filled with flames. The whole of the abbey is a crucible. Every window burning. Except one. Mine! And that one is black as night. It is the window which the abbot flung open in his dramatic act of ventilation and which I had forgotten to close. *I had broken a rule.* (79)

CHAPTER 6

Reading: Nature to Advantage Dress'd

The reader of the text could be compared to an idle subject (a subject having relaxed his "imaginary"): this fairly empty subject strolls along the side of a valley at the bottom of which runs a *wadi* (I use *wadi* here to stress a certain feeling of unfamiliarity). What he sees is multiple and irreducible; it emerges from the substances and levels that are heterogeneous and disconnected: lights, colors, vegetation, heat, air, bursts of noise, high-pitched bird calls, children's cries from the other side of the valley, paths, gestures, clothing and close and distant inhabitants. All these *occurrences* are partially identifiable: they proceed from known codes, but their combination is unique, founding the stroll in difference that can be repeated only as difference. This is what happens in the case of the Text: it can be itself only in its difference.

—Roland Barthes, "From Work to Text"

To round out a book that uses *ethos, pathos, logos,* and *form* as a structuring rubric, the last chapter should deal with *style.*

In a well-known essay ("What Is Stylistics and Why Are They Saying Such Terrible Things About It?"), Stanley Fish debunks stylisticians who would attribute independent meaning to linguistic facts, namely, the surface structure of sentences or the hypothetical transformational history by which those sentences were generated, for, in any case, he says, the facts "will mean differently in different circumstances," and using them to prove this about the prose style of Jonathan Swift, that about "The Secret Sharer," and the other about a story by John Updike is "a game that is just too easy to play" (77).

And it is a game that I will not play in this chapter, for my interest is in the reading experience provided by four books: *Arctic Dreams,* by Barry Lopez; *Pilgrim at Tinker Creek,* by Annie Dillard; *Desert Solitaire,* by Edward Abbey; and *The Snow Leopard,* by Peter Matthiessen. These are "nature" studies in the tradition from Thoreau to Mary Austin, Farley Mowat, Wallace Stegner, Ann Zwinger, and Dian Fossey, to name but a few of the many nature writers in the North American tradition. If you long for statistics and parsing, the chapter is bound to disappoint you.

In his introduction to *The John McPhee Reader,* William Howarth illustrates the difficulty of drawing the boundary between style and subject. McPhee's style, says Howarth, is "fresh, strong, unaffected, and yet entirely idiosyncratic," like his description of Bill Bradley playing basketball: "taut, impersonal, yet carrying values like endurance, precision, solitude, success" (xxiv). Another characteristic of McPhee's style is "persistent good humor" (xxv).

As vague as these characterizations are (and as much as one might wish for sufficient examples to illustrate the tautness, impersonality, and so forth), I am quite willing to accept them, for they point to Howarth's reaction to the attitudinal tenor of the author's work. They also, of course, raise the question "Where does manner end and matter begin?"

As will become obvious, if my position has not been evident from the beginning of this book, I am a relativist. In regard to "style," I can say that the least interesting aspect of *that* subject is what you can say about the language system itself. Style is my attitude toward the text: laconic, good natured, terse, ambling, etc. In a thoroughgoing account of the style of a text, I would, of course, deal with the language system (syntax, diction, and figures). However, the language system is polluted by subject matter, and a relative clause about winning millions in the California lottery and a relative clause about losing one's life's savings in a stock scam are radically different *stylistically* even though they may be identical structurally. Finally, of course, style exists in the reader, not in data culled from the page, and a relative clause about losing one's life savings in a stock scam might be, depending on the reader, either hilariously funny or tragic.

Though I will not analyze the styles of the four authors, it will become evident through quotations from their works that no predominant syntactic features mark their writing. Barry Lopez has a precocious-schoolboy fascination with big words (within two pages, "*lacustrine* soil," growing in lakes; "*lamellation* of snow," formed into thin, flat scales; "*irenic,* northern summers," peaceful; and "*salutary* existence"); otherwise, the diction of the authors—except for necessary technical terms (and there are relatively few of them)—does not call attention to itself.

The "stylistic" feature that they share is attention to concrete details, but the use they make of these details differs among the four. On the spectrum from psychology of information to psychology of form, Barry Lopez is at the sinistral end with his fascinatingly *informative* account of the arctic. Edward Abbey is somewhere in the middle, his book a hybrid. Peter Matthiessen and Annie Dillard are so lyrical that the information they supply is only a vehicle for the attitudes that they dance.

As is my wont, I will restate the point in more homely terms: If you want to learn about the arctic, go to Barry Lopez; if you want a passionate account of the desert in southeastern Utah, turn to Edward Abbey. But what essential knowledge do you gain from Annie Dillard? About Annie Dillard and how she learns to "see." Or from Peter Matthiessen? About Peter Matthiessen's tragic quest.

I will use *Pilgrim at Tinker Creek* and *Desert Solitaire* contrapuntally in a discussion that centers on *Arctic Dreams* and *The Snow Leopard*.

This chapter reiterates the premise that what we have been calling "the literature of fact" has been devalued. Two categories of texts have been created: "imaginative literature" (or, if you will, simply "literature"), which constitutes nearly the whole enterprise of the literary establishment; and all of the other, though, of course, fringe cases, such as *Walden* create a certain blurring of the distinctions.

However, if we talk not about kinds of texts, but about *kinds of reading experience,* as do, for instance, Louise Rosenblatt and Roland Barthes, we can gain a new perspective on literature, for it is only cultural bias that makes a work such as *The Snow Leopard,* which we will discuss in some detail hereafter, less satisfying esthetically than, say, *Moby Dick.* "Esthetic" reading comes about through *immersion,* and we immerse ourselves in *unified* texts, whether "factual" or fictive.

The two kinds of unity are lyric, created and maintained by the theme of the work and the writer's attitude, as in *Pilgrim at Tinker Creek,* and narrative, created by plot, as in *The Snow Leopard* (which is contrasted with the disunified *Arctic Dreams*).

Toward Rehabilitating the Literature of Fact

Devaluation of the Literature of Fact

The major theme of both *Roderick Hudson* and *The Tragic Muse* is the conflict between the world of art and the "real" world. In *The Tragic Muse,* Nick Dormer, the son of an influential British politician, runs for the House of Commons, and under the aegis of a wealthy, beautiful widow, Julia Dallow, gains the seat for Harsh. His patron and his father's old friend, the wealthy Mr. Carteret, promises Nick a substantial endowment when he secures his position in public life and society by marrying Mrs. Dallow. Nick, however, choosing to become a painter, resigns his seat in the house and thus renounces his chance to become a significant public figure, a decision that loses him Mrs. Dallow and her fortune as well as the promised legacy from Mr. Carteret (though at the conclusion, James hints that Nick will be able both to maintain his artistic career and to secure Julia as his wife).

The other couple in the novel are Miriam Rooth, a young actress who gains sudden and great acclaim, and Peter Sherringham, a rising young diplomat with a fascination for the theater. In this case, Peter wants Miriam to give up her career on the stage, to marry one who is certain to become a leading personage in the affairs of the nation. Miriam turns the tables on Peter, asking him to give up diplomacy for a life in the theater with her, which he is unwilling to do.

The almost obsessive recapitulation of the art vs. life conflict is, of course, simply a fictionalization of the conflict that Henry James lived through. His father was skeptical about artists and writers, and his venerated older brother, William, seems to have been afflicted by "a certain blindness to the laws of art that dictated his brother's life" (Edel, *Henry James: A Life* 162). In a letter, Henry wrote deprecatingly of his chosen career: "'To produce some little exemplary works of art is my narrow and lowly dream'" (Edel 152).

In Henry James we can read an attitude of both apology and defensiveness; he gave himself to literary art completely, yet he did not announce himself as an unacknowledged legislator of the world.

The same attitude permeates modern theories of literature, which are, in effect, apologies. We have seen Wellek and Warren on the defensive, assuring us that literary scholarship has "its own valid methods which are not those of the natural sciences but are nevertheless intellectual methods" (16). Their next move, of course, is to reduce the object of study to language: "Language is the material of literature as stone or bronze is of sculpture, paints of pictures, or sounds of music. But one should realize that language is not mere inert matter like stone but is itself a creation of man and is thus charged with the cultural heritage of a linguistic group" (22).

This extraordinary metaphor puts Wellek and Warren in a bizarre position: literary study is, on the one hand, a branch of linguistics (as sculpture must be a branch of petrology or metallurgy) and, on the other, a historical discipline. In either case, the study of literature does not include rhetoric (except in the narrow, post-Ramistic view of rhetoric as the study of tropes).

And we have also seen the move that Northrop Frye made in *Anatomy:*

In literature, questions of fact or truth are subordinated to the primary literary aim of producing a structure of words for its own sake, and the sign- values of symbols are subordinated to their importance as a structure of interconnected motifs. Wherever we have an autonomous verbal structure of this kind, we have literature. Wherever this autonomous structure is lacking, we have language, words used instrumentally to help human consciousness do or understand something else. (74)

We are left, then, with a surplus of guilt and two categories of texts: guilt because we value texts that presumably are not useful—at least not directly so—in the world outside art; two categories of texts because some are autonomous and some are not.

Immersion and Unified Texts

However, distinguishing two categories of *reading* is quite different from dividing texts into two classes, literature and non-literature. In the first chapter, I discussed Louise Rosenblatt's distinction between two kinds of reading, *efferent,* in which "the reader's attention is focused primarily on what will remain as the residue *after* the reading—the information to be acquired, the logical solution to a problem, the actions to be carried out" (23)—and *esthetic,* wherein "the reader's primary concern is with what happens *during* the actual reading event" (24). As I said, any text can be read either efferently or esthetically, though some texts have more potentiality for esthetic reading, a point that has been, of course, one of the purposes of this book to explain. I would argue that there is no reason, except cultural bias, for our having a less esthetically satisfying experience in reading, for example, Jay Martin's superb biography of Henry Miller (*Always Merry and Bright*) than in reading the fictional life of Stephen Dedalus.

An interesting and perverse notion here arises: that there is really no difference between literature and, for instance, literary criticism since all types of texts can be experienced esthetically, exactly

Barthes's point about text, which is *"experienced only in an activity, a production.* It follows that Text cannot stop, at the end of library shelf, for example; the constitutive movement of the Text is a *traversal [traverse]*: it can cut across a work, several works" ("From Work to Text" 75).

We can immerse ourselves in any kind of text, including one that develops an argument (e.g., in my own reading, Derrida's *Of Grammatology,* Jaynes' *The Origin of Consciousness in the Breakdown of the Bicameral Mind,* John Robert Ross's "On Declarative Sentences," Stephen Jay Gould's "Natural Selection and the Human Brain: Darwin *vs.* Wallace"), and this immersion is an esthetic response in that the text is an "autonomous structure," not, *during the reading,* words used instrumentally to help human consciousness do or understand something else.

To state the point again: we can become immersed in any text that has subject matter meaningful to us and that is (or that we take to be) unified.

In *The Ethics of Reading,* J. Hillis Miller, extrapolating from Kant's *Grundlegung zur Metaphysik der Sitten* (*Foundations of the Metaphysics of Morals*) (1785), speaks of the paradoxical relationship between constraints and freedom in reading:

> By "the ethics of reading," the reader will remember, I mean that aspect of the act of reading in which there is a response to the text that is both necessitated, in the sense that it is a response to an irresistible demand, and free, in the sense that I must take responsibility for my response and for the further effects, "interpersonal," institutional, social, political, or historical, of my act of reading, for example as that act takes the form of teaching or of published commentary on a given text. What happens when I read *must* happen, but I must acknowledge it as *my* act of reading, though just what the "I" is or becomes in this transaction is another question. (43)

However, we can easily conceive of reading acts that are *not* inevitable—that result, as a matter of fact, from conscious choice. As an example, take the following passage from *The Ethics of Reading:* "No doubt the political and the ethical are always intimately intertwined, but an ethical act that is fully determined by political considerations or responsibilities is no longer ethical" (4). Like many passages in *every* book, this one does not "compute," but, rather, creates a paradox. If an act is fully determined by political considerations, it is not, by the conditions of Miller's own argument, an ethical act but a political one and was such from its inception. In other words, we have here a fissure in the argument, and with various tools (crow bars, sledge hammers, pickaxes) and explosives we can widen the fissure until the text falls asunder. Or we can attempt to "bridge" the fissure with the implications that the text itself provides and with our own knowledge of the author, the subject he is handling, and the category of texts to which this one belongs.

In choosing a passage from *The Ethics of Reading* as my example, I do not mean to imply that the book is mortally flawed; it is, in fact, an important and convincing statement. However, one point needs stressing: since fissures crisscross the territory of every text, except possibly the briefest and most rudimentary, every text is vulnerable. The primary ethical decision a reader makes is the choice between attempting to assemble or to disassemble a text.

In fact, both the reality and cooperative principles (discussed in chapter 2) are based on the premise that readers assume texts can be unified and will yield the author's semantic intention. (The reality principle, it will be recalled, is simply a reader's belief that the text is referring to a situation that he or she can make sense of, and the cooperative principle, as we have seen, is the reader's assumption that the writer is trying to tell the truth, to provide all needed information and no more, to be relevant, and to be as clear as possible.) If in a given instance the reader does not give assent to the reality principle, he or she will not attempt to read the text. For the text to make sense, the reader must rationalize any apparent violations of the cooperative principle; if such rationalization seems impossible, the reader will abandon the text. However, one hardly needs scientific or statistical proof for the axiom that most readers *do* undertake such rationalization most of the time.

Reasons for disassembling the text are, of course, as varied as reasons for assembling it. The "logic" may appear to be so flawed as to be irreparable, in which case the reader has decided that the fissures are unbridgeable. The reader may not be able to relate parts (symbols, images, scenes, characters) to a whole and thus may feel that the text is not tightly unified or unifiable.

A common misinterpretation of deconstructionism holds that writing is constructive, and reading is deconstructive; however, if the reader does not first *construct* a global representation of a text's meaning, there is nothing to deconstruct. Thus, it is more accurate to say that the writer constructs and the reader *re*constructs, and just as the writer can revise, so can the reader *de*construct.

In a particularly evocative passage, Wolfgang Iser describes what
I would call the experience of immersion in a text.

> It is clear . . . that throughout the reading process there is a continual
> interplay between modified expectations and transformed memories. How-
> ever, the text itself does not formulate expectations or their modification;
> nor does it specify how the connectability of memories is to be implemented.
> This is the province of the reader himself, and so here we have a first
> insight into how the synthesizing activity of the reader enables the text to
> be translated and transferred to his own mind. This process of translation
> also shows up the basic hermeneutic structure of reading. Each sentence
> correlate contains what one might call *a hollow section*, which looks forward
> to the next correlate, and a retrospective section, which answers the expecta-
> tions of the preceding sentence (now part of the remembered background).
> Thus every moment of reading is a dialectic of protension and retention,
> conveying a future horizon yet to be occupied, along with a past (and
> continually fading) horizon already filled; the wandering viewpoint carves
> its passage through both at the same time and leaves them to merge together
> in its wake. (*The Act of Reading* 112)

Translated into linguistic terms, the passage is saying that readers
must continually use their world knowledge in order to deal with
implicatures—that is, *presuppositions* (knowledge taken as given) and
inferences (knowledge deduced from the text, but not stated directly). The image is that of gaps which the reader must bridge.

Simpleminded examples are easy to find or cook up. In an example that is now famous, the linguist Charles Fillmore speaks of two
signs on the wall of a swimming pool being taken as a coherent text.
One sign says, "Use restrooms, not pool." The other says, "Pool for
members' use only." The crucial presupposition here is that some
people do "use" pools rather than going to the restroom. The
inference that can be deduced from the text is that members, and
only members, are free to "use" the pool (Tannen 79). The reader
bridges the *hollow section* with world knowledge, thus creating a
coherent (and humorous) text.

Iser's explanation of this phenomenon has resonances of that
community who value literature defined as imaginative works. It is
worthwhile to let two psycholinguists give the same explanation, not
only for the added understanding of the principle gained thereby,
but for the stark contrast in ways of saying and knowing. Herbert
H. Clark and Eve V. Clark explain the coherence of these two
sentences: *Patience walked into a room. The chandeliers burned brightly.*

By a proposal of H. Clark and Haviland's . . . listeners get over such impasses by building bridging assumptions. Whenever they cannot identify an antecedent, they suppose they are expected to do so indirectly—at least if the speaker is being cooperative. In [the example sentence], they note that if they assumed that the room had chandeliers, they would have a direct antecedent for *the chandeliers*. Since this is an assumption the speaker could expect them to grasp, they add this bridging assumption, or *implicature*, to memory as part of what the speaker meant to convey. Thus, they add to memory not only the information in [the example], but also the implicature in [the following]: The room referred to by *a room* had chandeliers in it. (97)

But we can move from the realm of abstract explanations, such as Iser's, and of laboratory experiments, such as those of Clark and Clark, to living texts and find that when we are unable to bridge gaps, the structure develops fissures and begins to crumble.

In *Desert Solitaire*, Abbey tells of a roundup in which he participated—basically a vivid tale of the Old West in the 1950s. One old cow simply lay down in the tamarisk, and Abbey was forced to fight his way through brush, gnats, and yellow-backed flies to get her out.

At last, groaning and farting with exaggerated self-pity, she hoisted her rear end, then her front end, and plodded off to rejoin the gang. When I got back to my horse I was too tired to climb immediately into the saddle; it seemed easier for a while to walk and lead the horse. (103)

Well and good. The mood and scene are vividly established. And then:

Second movement, seventh symphony, Beethoven again—the slow, ponderous dirge. Had the sun moved at all: Not that I could tell. But as I came up with the others, Viviano [another cowboy], grinning through his dusty face, yelled at me:
"Around the bend, only nine son of bitch more, we get the Jesus Christ out of here." (103)

I am unable to bridge the gap between farting cows and Beethoven and that between cursing cowboys and the Seventh Symphony. In other words, the principle of "bridging assumptions" and of gaps (per Iser) has wider implications than either the literary theorist or the psycholinguists have indicated. I am unable to build on the basis of either syllogistic or qualitative progression.

In his introduction, Abbey tells us that *Desert Solitaire* is disunified, a collage:

There was time enough for once to do nothing, or next to nothing, and most of the substance of this book is drawn, sometimes direct and unchanged, from the pages of the journals I kept and filled through the undivided, seamless days of those marvelous summers [spent as a ranger at the Arches in Utah]. The remainder of the book consists of digressions and excursions into ideas and places that border in varied ways upon that central season in the canyonlands. (x)

But view it from the standpoint of *ethos*, and suddenly it comes together, like a movie of Humpty Dumpty's fall run backwards. That is, the book becomes the expression of an author or persona and simply reflects his diversity of mood, attention, tastes, ideas, and so on.

Facts and the Dancing of Attitudes

The thirteenth chapter of Dillard's *Pilgrim at Tinker Creek* is exceptionally informative, packed as it is with facts (or what I take to be facts, not fictions) about insects.

There is an insect order that consists entirely of parasitic insects called, singly and collectively, stylops, which is interesting because of the grotesquerie of its forms and its effects. Stylops parasitize divers other insects such as leaf hoppers, ants, bees, and wasps. The female spends her entire life inside the body of her host, with only the tip of her bean-shaped body protruding. She is a formless lump, having no wings, legs, eyes, or antennae; her vestigial mouth and anus are tiny, degenerate, and nonfunctional. She absorbs food—her host—through the skin of her abdomen, which is "inflated, white, and soft." (237–38)

And, indeed, we learn about stylops sex life—"The male inserts his sperm into the brood canal, whence it flows into her disorganized body and fertilizes the eggs that are floating there" (238)—and the effect of this parasite on the hosts: "Their colors brighten. The gonads of males and females are 'destroyed,' and they not only lose their secondary sexual characteristics, they actually acquire those of the opposite sex" (238).

In a way this radical factual particularity is like the Baedeker effect in Irving Stone's fictionalized biographies, providing information that we find interesting in and of itself, a playful factuality, literary "Trivial Pursuit" or "Jeopardy." But, of course, even the most enthusiastic fans of Irving Stone would be ill-advised to read *Passions of the Mind* only for what it can tell them about psychoanalysis, and no one would recommend *Pilgrim at Tinker Creek* as an introduction to entomology.

The Baedeker sections of *Passions of the Mind* are, I argued, unintegrated—that is, they appeal to the "psychology of information," but have little qualitative relationship to the acts in the book. The value of the "facts" in *Pilgrim at Tinker Creek* is precisely qualitative, serving as the basis for a meditation on parasitism, "a sort of rent, paid by all creatures who live in the real world with us now" (239). In presentational literature, facts have value not as information (or at least not solely as information), but as manifestations of attitude or as the basis for a meditative discussion, as when Annie Dillard begins to extract the "meaning" from her detailed information concerning insects:

> The creator is no puritan. A creature need not work for a living; creatures may simply steal and such and be blessed for all that with a share—an enormous share—of the sunlight and air. There is something that profoundly fails to be exuberant about these crawling, translucent lice and white, fat-bodied grubs, but there is an almost manic exuberance about a creator who turns them out, creature after creature, and sets them buzzing and lurking and flying and swimming about. (239)

Reading Two Books About Nature

The Informative Dreams of Barry Lopez

Arctic Dreams is a wonderful book to read and a difficult book to discuss. The subtitle, "Imagination and Desire in a Northern Landscape," creates the first problem, asking the reader, I think, to put the book in the same category as *Walden* when, in fact, it is a good deal more like *Coming Into the Country,* John McPhee's superb book about Alaska. Lopez promises one sort of book, but delivers another. (In just the same way, the advertising blurb on the cover of *Coming Into the Country* makes a false promise: "A voyage of spirit and mind into America's last great wilderness—Alaska.")

Clinging pertinaciously to one of the distinctions that are the basis for this book, I would argue that *Coming Into the Country* and *Arctic Dreams* are discursive; that they are not presentational or essentially lyrical. The "Prologue" of *Arctic Dreams*, the history of Pond's Bay, Baffin Island, is pure McPhee. "On a warm summer day in 1823, the *Cumbrian*, a 360-ton British whaler, sailed into the waters off Pond's Bay (now Pond Inlet), northern Baffin Island, after a short excursion to the north" (1). And here is a typical McPhee beginning: "One morning in the Alaskan autumn, a small sharp-nosed helicopter, on its way to a rendezvous, flew south from Fairbanks with three passengers" (*Coming Into the Country*, Book II, 97).

But, as a matter of fact, Lopez, unlike McPhee, begins his book with a "Preface," in which he explains that the book "finds its origins in two moments" (xix). One was an encounter with a defiant horned lark "no bigger than my fist" (xix), and the other was a visit to the grave of Edward Israel who had died in 1884 on an expedition to the arctic (xx–xxi). The first incident symbolizes, for Lopez, "sublime innocence" and the second, the struggle "to come to terms with the Far North" (xxii).

Lopez is setting us up for an inward journey, what might be called a "meditation," or at least a mental odyssey: "The mind, full of curiosity and analysis, disassembles a landscape and then reassembles the pieces—the nod of a flower, the color of the night sky, the murmur of an animal—trying to fathom its geography. At the same time the mind is trying to find a place within the land, to discover a way to dispel its own sense of estrangement" (xxii–xxiii). After having read *Arctic Dreams*, however, one concludes I think that *logos* dominates *ethos*, and in the lyric *ethos* predominates.

Arctic Dreams is a big book (464 pages) and, in some ways, encyclopedic, with chapters on the animals (e.g., musk ox, polar bear) and places (e.g., Banks Island, Lancaster Sound, Pingok Island) of the arctic. For example, on the coloration of polar bears:

The ivory and pearl shading we see in a polar bear's fur is caused by the refraction of sunlight (the same phenomenon that makes clouds appear white) in its guard hairs. The hair itself is optically transparent, or colorless. The brightest whites show up in the spring molt, the purest of these being those of young cubs. With exposure to sunlight, the hairs take on a subtle coloring; soft yellowish tones appear on the hips, along the flanks, and down the legs—a pale lemon wash, apricot yellows, cream buffs, straw whites. The tones deepen each year as the animal ages. In the low sunlight of a fall afternoon an older male's fur might suggest the yellow golds of ripe wheat. (84)[1]

Lopez is a master at depicting scenes, both closeups and panoramas.

During those summers I found, too, the molted feathers of ducks washed up in great wrack lines, in heaps, on the beach. Undisturbed in shallow waters on the lagoon side, I found hoofprints of caribou, as sharp as if the animals had stepped there in fresh clay only moments before. (254)

In the sometimes disconcerting summary which is a photograph, Pingok Island would seem bleak and forsaken. In winter it disappears beneath whiteness, a flat white plain extending seaward into the Beaufort Sea ice and landward without a border into the tundra of the coastal plain. The island emerges in June, resplendent with flowers and insects and birds, only to disappear again in a few months beneath the first snowstorms. (255)

Lopez packs his book with not only fact, but what might be called general cultural knowledge: comments on structuralism, several explorations of historiography, and an unfortunately overenthusiastic commentary on the language theories of Benjamin Lee Whorf, from whose work Lopez concludes that because of the nature of the Hopi language, "All else being equal, a Hopi child would have little difficulty comprehending the theory of relativity in his own language, while an American child could more easily master history" (274). This is not the place to explain why Lopez is misguided about Hopi (and English, for that matter), but my friend and colleague Ed Finegan, a linguist, remarked that Einstein's native and second languages would be fairly convincing evidence against Lopez.

Books by naturalists often and understandably involve walks, which become the structural framework of the narrative and symbolic of some kind of quest. As we shall see, *The Snow Leopard* is a day-by-day account of a walk in quest of soul's peace; *Pilgrim at Tinker Creek* tells of walk after walk, in the course of which Annie Dillard learns to "see"; Edward Abbey's walks in *Desert Solitaire* are subjective guided tours. The walk in chapter 7 of *Arctic Dreams* ("The Country of the Mind") demonstrates why the book fails to deliver on its promise to become lyrically presentational.

[1] Interestingly, just after I read this passage, I visited the Los Angeles Zoo and saw polar bears anew, through the lens provided by *Arctic Dreams*. That these magnificent creatures should be confined to a small, concrete "environment" must sadden anyone who would enjoy *Arctic Dreams*, which, like all good books, gives the reader new ways of seeing.

In literature (and, I think, in actual fact), the solitary walk involves two sorts of intense mental awareness, each of which largely precludes the other: first, with the *walker's* sensory impressions involved (including the kinesthetic) and, second, with the *walker's* preoccupations (ideas, troubles, triumphs, longings, memories). *Ethos* is always foregrounded. For example, walking with Edward Abbey:

> I walk out the foot trail to Double Arch and the Windows. The wind moans a dreary tune under the overhanging coves, among the holes in the rock, and through the dead pinyon pines. The sky is obscure and yellow but the air in this relatively sheltered place among the rocks is still clear. A few birds dart about: black-throated sparrows, the cliff swallows, squawking magpies in their handsome academic dress of black and white. In the dust and on the sand dunes I can read the passage of other creatures, from the big track of a buck to the tiny prints of bird, mice, lizards, and insects. Hopefully I look for sign of bobcat or coyote but find none.
>
> We need more predators. The sheepmen complain, it is true, that the coyotes eat some of their lambs. This is true but do they eat enough? I mean, enough lambs to keep the coyotes sleek, healthy and well fed. That is my concern. (*Desert Solitaire* 35)

The narrative moves seamlessly, by free association, from the sense experience to the thought. And this unity of image and exposition is essential if the text is to be a lyric.

Now we will follow Barry Lopez on his walk (pages 257–74). We start, as we must, in the realm of the image: "As I step out of our small cabin on Pingok Island, the undistinguished plain of tundra spreads before me to the south and east. A few glaucous gulls rise from the ground and drop back, and I feel the cold, damp air, like air from a refrigerator, against my cheeks. A few yards from the door, stark and alone on the tundra, a female common eider lies dead" (257). After another half page of imagistic narrative, Lopez begins to muse about the nature of time and to suggest that "if one is dressed well and carrying a little food, and has the means to secure more food and to construct shelter, the mind is that much more free to work with the senses in an appreciation of the country" (258–59). And back to the images of the walk, even to the change in the sound of the walker's footfall as he steps from damp ground to wet.

But now comes such an abrupt change that the fabric of mood and tone is rent: "The western history of Pingok Island comprises few events. John Franklin, a young British naval officer, led an overland party almost this far west from the mouth of the Mackenzie in 1826, trying for a Rendezvous at Point Barrow, 250 miles farther on" (261). And there follow four pages of history and anthropology. It is now *logos* that propels the reader.

On page 271 we are briefly back to the meditative walk, but then go on to an exceptionally interesting discussion of what might be called natural epistemology: "What one thinks of any region, while traveling through, is the result of at least three things: what one knows, what one imagines, and how one is disposed" (271). Pages 273 and 274 end the walk back at the cabin.

Arctic Dreams is an exceptionally interesting book, yet, as I have been attempting to explain, it lacks the intensity that the lyric ratio, that of agent-scene, creates. It is too disunified to sustain itself.

Peter Matthiessen's Lyric Trek

The Snow Leopard is a magnificent achievement, having all the power of a great novel with a first-person narrator as well as the inherent appeal of informativeness. One reads the book as "fact," not fiction, but becomes totally immersed esthetically. Three simultaneous movements provide structure for *The Snow Leopard:* through time, space, and free association of ideas. We are continually reminded of the temporality since the book is in the form of a journal, starting with the entry of September 28, 1973, and ending with the entry of December 1, the same year (though a brief anachronistic interpolation takes the account to December 10).

The story records a field trip to an area in Nepal, near the border of Tibet, that Matthiessen took with the zoologist George Schaller to study bharal or Himalayan blue sheep.

Even though the books are different in structure, the ingredients of *The Snow Leopard* are like those of *Arctic Dreams*, narrative pausing for the "radical particularity" of images, and information about flora and fauna leading to philosophical musings. The great difference between them is the way in which the particulars "add up" in *The Snow Leopard*. *Arctic Dreams* has something of the disunity of Irving Stone's *Passions of the Mind*, whereas *The Snow Leopard* has the total unity necessary for a work of art to achieve maximum power.[2]

2 A book in many ways like *The Snow Leopard* is Robert M. Pirsig's *Zen and the Art of Motorcycle Maintenance: An Inquiry Into Values,* which chonicles a cross-country motorcycle journey that Pirsig took with his son. Though I think that the book is clearly excellent, it does not achieve the total unity that gives *The Snow Leopard* its overwhelming power.

The fallacy of division is the assumption that the whole will have the attributes of its parts—so that if the parts A, B, C, D . . . of X are all beautiful, X will naturally be beautiful. The parts of *The Snow Leopard* are, indeed, exceptionally satisfying, viewed separately and discretely, and the work as a totality is exceptionally satisfying because of the way in which the parts constitute a coherent whole.

The theme of the book is the search for enlightenment, the diverse elements of the narrative relating always to that theme, building it, giving it the depth and complexity of a lived drama.

The Snow Leopard is, of course, a travel book, and like all good travel writers, Matthiessen gives us a vivid sense of scene. The journey begins, at the end of September, in the lowlands of Nepal, where "Green village compounds, set about with giant banyans and old stone pools and walls, are cropped to lawn by water buffalo and cattle; the fresh water and soft shade give them the harmony of parks" (14–15). Children play in the warm sun, "and women roll clothes on rocks at the village fountain and pound grain in stone mortars, and from all sides come reassuring dung smells and chicken clatter and wafts of fire smoke from the low hearths" (15). Here is fecund easiness, life growing like the "yellow-flowered pumpkin vines" and the maize and the rice "spread to dry on broad straw mats" and the banana and papaya trees. However, the way lies upward and northward toward the snowy peaks of the Himalayas.

The scene becomes progressively more austere, mystical. After a long climb, "A pine forest drifts by in breaths of mist, and on the mountain face just opposite, seen through shifting clouds, ribbons of water turn from white to brown as they gather up soil in the fall to the roaring rivers. On a corner of the trail is a weird shrine where horns of many slaughtered goats are piled high in a kind of altar, with red ribbons tied to branches of the trees" (37).

The climax of the journey and of the scenic progression is in the vicinity of Crystal Mountain, where, on an adjoining peak, Matthiessen has found a place for meditation, "a broken rock outcrop like an altar set into the hillside, protected from all but the south wind by shards of granite and dense thorn" (217). "Now the mountains all around me take on life; the Crystal Mountain moves. Soon there comes the murmur of the torrent, from far away below under the ice: it seems impossible that I can hear the sound. Even in the windlessness, the sound of rivers comes and goes and falls and rises, like the wind itself" (217). This is the scene of the epiphany, but we will return to discuss that moment hereafter. The point is that *scene* in *The Snow Leopard* is never gratuitous and never merely for information, but is always the right setting for the *acts* that make up the narrative. As Kenneth Burke put it, in drama the scene and the acts that take place therein should be consistent, unless the purpose is comic or grotesque (*Grammar* 3–7).

A prominent motif of *The Snow Leopard* is natural history, and like all good natural historians (Darwin, Muir), Matthiessen gives vivid accounts of the flora and especially the fauna of the regions he traverses. The unbelievably difficult trek—through snow-clogged mountain passes, often with nothing to eat except a "white diet" of rice and millet—is a quest symbolized by two animals: the bharal, or Himalayan blue sheep, which George Schaller has set out to study, and the near mythic snow leopard, which Matthiessen hopes to see.

Schaller is " 'single-minded, not easy to know' and 'a stern pragmatist,' unable to muster up much grace in the face of unscientific attitudes; he takes a hard-eyed look at almost everything" (4). His purpose is to confirm his belief that bharal is the common ancestor of both sheep and goats, but that the animal itself is more of a goat than a sheep (3). Schaller undergoes the severe test of the journey to establish zoological fact.

And Matthiessen's reason for the trek? In Kathmandu he and Schaller had visited with a young biologist, who automatically comprehended Schaller's motive. But Matthiessen's? "How could I say that I wished to penetrate the secrets of the mountains in search of something still unknown that, like the yeti, might well be missed for the very fact of searching?" (131). How, indeed, could Matthiessen advance a logical reason for the rigors and hazards of the expedition? Could he claim that the possibility of glimpsing a snow leopard was explanation enough?

As the bharal are symbols of rationality, so the snow leopard becomes the symbol of suprarationality, and in the psychic territory between rationality and suprarationality is the legend of yeti. The evidence in favor of its existence is strong enough to convince even the skeptical Schaller—and yet, if yeti exists, why have all expeditions pursuing these creatures failed (128–31)?

And the wolves at Crystal Mountain. Schaller and Matthiessen watch the pack attempt to bring down a bharal, which narrowly escapes capture. So tense is the drama that "the whole mountain is taut; the silence rings. The sheep's flanks quake, and the wolves are panting; otherwise, all is still, as if the arrangement of pale shapes held the world together. Then I breathe, and the mountain breathes, setting the world in motion once again" (204). The stoical Schaller says that this one incident is enough to justify the whole trip.

The Snow Leopard is a documentary, and like all good documentary storytellers (Parkman, Dana, the Mark Twain of *Roughing It* and *Life on the Mississippi*), Matthiessen gives us infinitely fascinating characters.

For example, there is old Bimbahadur. One morning, Schaller and Matthiessen find bare human footprints in the snow. " 'Yeti,' says GS, sardonic" (101). But even for Schaller, the footprints are unsettling, ominous. And then down the narrow valley toward them comes a weird figure, gesturing wildly, uttering screams unheard because of the torrent through the narrow col. Matthiessen assumes the wild person is a *sennin*, a Himalayan mountain lunatic, but he turns out to be old Bimbahadur, the bearer, gesturing to indicate the direction of the trail the party would follow that day. Matthiessen learns, astonishingly, that Bimbahadur "had walked three miles upriver in the rain, the night before, to sleep alone in a cave of his own ken, and was now on his way down again to fetch his load!" (101).

Of the people on the journey, one character, aside from the narrator, becomes progressively more interesting and more central to the book's theme: the Sherpa Tukten, who, unlike the other porters, stays with the expedition from beginning to end.

We first meet Tukten, "a wiry small man with Mongol eyes and outsized ears," in the green, edenic lowlands, about which he makes the comment, " 'Too many hot' " (15).

He is an extraordinarily complex being, radiating "that inner quiet which is often associated with spiritual attainment, but perhaps his attainment is a dark one" (53). In fact, he becomes Matthiessen's *Doppelgänger*, his secret sharer, known, perhaps, from a previous life (54). Encountering the calm gaze of Tukten, Matthiessen finds, as in a spiritual mirror, his own shortcomings, "all this is hollow in myself, all that is greedy, angry, and unwise" (54).

And he becomes more than one person's secret sharer, for in his possible many lives, he has been everywhere and thus knows all humanity, is the *Doppelgänger* of Everyman, is "touched by what the Tibetans call 'the crazy wisdom': he is free" (88). He was, all along, the teacher that Matthiessen had hoped to find, and even from the holiest of beings, the Lama of the Crystal Monastery, Matthiessen has less to learn than from Tukten's crazy wisdom. "In his life in the moment, in his freedom from attachments, in the simplicity of his everyday example, Tukten has taught me over and over, he is the teacher I had hoped to find" (327), thoroughly human, an amalgam of good and bad.

If the dénouement, however, were so pat, solving the mystery that the narrative attempts to convey, we would conclude, retrospectively, that the looming symbol of the snow leopard was inappropriate, a hoax, for Matthiessen did not glimpse this near mythic beast. We would also conclude that the motif of the book conveys a sanguine and easy life view, but from Tukten Matthiessen learns a final lesson.

At the hotel in Kathmandu, Matthiessen bids farewell to Tukten, with the promise to meet him after three days at the house of his father's sister. On the appointed day, Matthiessen bicycles to the outskirts of the city, and the book ends: "I walk my bicycle round and round the square, under the huge painted eyes [of the ancient shrine at Bodhinath], the nose like a great question mark, the wind-snapped pennants—Tukten? Tukten? But there is no answer, no one knows of Tukten Sherpa. Under the Bodhi Eye, I get on my bicycle again and return along the gray December roads to Kathmandu" (332).

Like a philosophical novel (for instance, *The Magic Mountain* or *Anna Karenina*—which is in so many ways akin to Matthiessen's masterpiece), *The Snow Leopard* embodies a *dialectic* concerning ideas, the doctrines of Buddhism: a dialectic because this noetic content develops through the *ethos* (the persona) of the narrator, through image and anecdote, and as part of the book's theme.

All of the exposition concerning Zen is alembicated in stunning moments during the narrative, as in the following account of the *sennin* dance, which is worth quoting at length:

The *sennin* [Himalayan mountain idiots] are a favorite subject of the great Zen painters, and sometimes their dance of life is staged against a landscape copied from these paintings, as if to suggest that such free beings perceive a master work in all of nature. Kanzan is studying a scroll while Jittoku leans easily on a broom; when the painting comes to life, the *sennin* begin the steps of a strange dance.

Soon Kanzan pauses, stands apart, gazing away into infinity. Jittoku, much moved, lifts his hands in an attitude of prayer and circles Kanzan with simple ceremony, kneeling beside him and lifting his gaze in reverent expectancy. Becoming aware of him, Kanzan inclines his head in acquiescence and kneels with dignity beside Jittoku. Together they open the scroll and hold it before them; the audience cannot see what is written, can only watch as the *sennin* read silently together. Now the two are struck by a perfect phrase, and they pause in the same instant to regard each other; the power of the revelation lifts them to their feet as they read on, eagerly nodding. Soon they finish, sigh, and turn away into the dance; for a moment, the scroll's face comes into view. It is pure white, void, without the smallest mark. Kanzan rolls it with great attention as Jittoku, smiling to himself, retrieves the broom.

Now Jittoku brings wine, but in his transport, he is holding the flagon upside down; the wine is gone. Not caring, he refills it from the stream, and the *sennin* are soon intoxicated on this pure water of high mountains. Kanzan must be supported in the dance, and for a time it seems that the two might sink away in drunken sleep. But they are summoned by the sublime song of a bird, and complete the dance by resuming the attitudes seen in the painting. Kanzan seems to smile, while Jittoku, regarding the audience for the first time, laughs silently, with all his heart. Before the audience can grasp what this might mean, the screen is drawn in a swift rush; there is only silence and the empty curtain. (89–90)

This anecdote summarizes and dramatizes the philosophical *Leitmotif* of the book. Through symbols and personal narrative, Matthiessen dramatizes the meaning of this *Leitmotif* to him.

In the firelight of a camp, he and Schaller were talking about the snow leopard, "wary and elusive to a magical degree" (158), never seen by those who search for it, but occasionally glimpsed almost accidentally by hunters who are watching a wild herd. We learn that very little is known about this mysterious cat (158–59), which has come to symbolize Matthiessen's spiritual quest. The leopard had undoubtedly been near the quester, had watched him, but he had never seen it.

And "though I am blind to it, the Truth is near in the reality of what I sit on—rocks" (217). Now he knows that "The mountains have no 'meaning,' they *are* meaning; the mountains *are*. The sun is round. I ring with life, and the mountains ring, and when I can hear it, there is a ringing that we share. I understand all this, not in my mind, but in my heart, knowing how meaningless it is to try to capture what cannot be expressed, knowing that mere words will remain when I read it all again, another day" (218).

The "message" of the book is cumulative, developing incrementally and recursively, as does the character of Tukten.

In 1971, Matthiessen and his wife, Deborah Love, had attended a weekend retreat, but meditating all day in the lotus posture was too rigorous for Deborah, and she decided to sit only on Sunday. When he returned from the Saturday session, Deborah looked exceptionally pretty, "But perhaps because I had been in meditation since before daybreak and my mind was clear, I saw at once that she was dying, and the certainty of this clairvoyance was so shocking that I had to feign emergency and push rudely into the bathroom, to get hold of myself so that I could speak" (110).

Thus, the theme of the book is the search for enlightenment, "a profound vision of his identity with universal life, past, present, and future, that keeps man from doing harm to others and sets him free from fear of birth-and-death" (18), which Matthiessen restates in a stunning image: "I wait, facing the north; instinct tells me to stand absolutely still. Cloud, mist, snow, and utter silence, utter solitude; extinction. Then, in the great hush, the clouds draw apart, revealing the vast Dhaulagiri snowfields. I breathe, mists swirl, and all has vanished—nothing! I make a small, involuntary bow" (76).

Textured as it is with detail, no book could be more sensuous than *The Snow Leopard*. Matthiessen tells us, "When one pays attention to the present, there is great pleasure in awareness of small things" (96), and "I can enjoy details" (175).

Under the eaves, on the clay windowsill, a flute, a wood comb, and a bright red pepper lie in happy composition. (33)

Cotoneaster of deep green, with its red berries, is the lone piece of color in the grayness. (75)

From the police house comes flat tin music from a small radio with weak batteries. (125)

The crowd gives off that heartening smell of uncultivated people the world over, an earthy but not sour smell of sweat and fire smoke and the oil of human leather. (148)

One could begin the interpretation of *The Snow Leopard* from other angles, reading the book, for instance, as a drama of the states of consciousness, from intense absorption in momentary detail, through rational thought, to the loss of individuality in union with the infinite: "The Universe itself is the scripture of Zen, for which religion is no more and no less than the apprehension of the infinite in every moment" (35). Whatever purpose brings the reader to *The Snow Leopard*, the reading experience is likely to be one of esthetic immersion.

References
Index

References

Abbey, Edward. *Desert Solitaire: A Season in the Wilderness.* New York: Ballantine, 1971.

Abbott, Jack Henry. *In the Belly of the Beast: Letters from Prison.* New York: Vintage, 1982.

Agee, James, and Walker Evans. *Let Us Now Praise Famous Men.* Boston: Houghton Mifflin, 1960.

Anderson, Chris. *Style as Argument: Contemporary American Nonfiction.* Carbondale: Southern Illinois UP, 1987.

Auerbach, Erich. *Mimesis: The Representation of Reality in Western Literature.* Trans. Willard Trask. Princeton: Princeton UP, 1968.

Augustine, Dorothy, and W. Ross Winterowd. "Speech Acts and the Reader-Writer Transaction." *Convergences: Transactions in Reading and Writing.* Ed. Bruce T. Petersen. Urbana: NCTE, 1986. 127–48.

Austin, J. L. *How to Do Things with Words.* Oxford: Oxford UP, 1962.

Barthes, Roland. "From Work to Text." *Textual Strategies.* Ed. Josué Harari. Ithaca: Cornell UP, 1979. 73–81.

Brodie, Fawn M. *Thomas Jefferson: An Intimate History.* New York: Bantam, 1975.

Brooks, Cleanth. *Modern Poetry and the Tradition.* Chapel Hill: U of North Carolina P, 1960.

Bryan, C. D. B. *Friendly Fire.* New York: Putnam, 1976.

Burke, Kenneth. *Attitudes Toward History.* 3rd ed. Berkeley and Los Angeles: U of California P, 1984.

———. *The Complete White Oxen.* Berkeley and Los Angeles: U of California P, 1968.

———. *Counter-Statement.* Los Altos, CA: Hermes, 1953.

———. *A Grammar of Motives.* Berkeley and Los Angeles: U of California P, 1969.

———. "Literature as Equipment for Living." *The Philosophy of Literary Form.* 1941. New York: Vintage, 1957. 253–62.

———. *The Philosophy of Literary Form.* 1941. New York: Vintage, 1957.

————. "Poetics in Particular, Language in General." *Language as Symbolic Action.* Berkeley and Los Angeles: U of California P, 1966. 25–43.

————. *A Rhetoric of Motives.* Berkeley and Los Angeles: U of California P, 1969.

————. *The Rhetoric of Religion.* Boston: Beacon, 1961.

Capote, Truman. *In Cold Blood: A True Account of a Murder and Its Consequences.* New York: Random House, 1965.

Clark, Herbert H., and Eve V. Clark. *Psychology and Language.* New York: Harcourt, 1977.

Coleridge, Samuel Taylor. *Biographia Literaria, or Biographical Sketches of My Literary Life and Opinions.* Ed. James Engell and W. Jackson Bate. Princeton: Princeton UP, 1983.

DeQuincey, Thomas. *Confessions of an English Opium-Eater and Other Writings.* Ed. Aileen Ward. New York: Carrol & Graff, 1985.

Didion, Joan. "Los Angeles Notebook." *Slouching Towards Bethlehem.* New York: Dell, 1968. 217–24.

————. "On Going Home." *Slouching Towards Bethlehem.* New York: Dell, 1968. 164–68.

Dillard, Annie. *Pilgrim at Tinker Creek.* New York: Bantam, 1975.

Dillon, George L. *Constructing Texts.* Bloomington: Indiana UP, 1981.

Drucker, Peter F. "Ernest Freedberg's World." *Adventures of a Bystander.* New York: Harper & Row, 1980. 187–212.

Eagleton, Terry. *Literary Theory: An Introduction.* Minneapolis: U of Minnesota P, 1983.

Eccles, John C. *Facing Reality.* Heidelberg and Berlin: Springer, 1970.

Edel, Leon. *Henry James: A Life.* New York: Harper & Row, 1985.

Eiseley, Loren. "The Angry Winter." *The Unexpected Universe.* New York: Harcourt, 1969. 93–119.

————."The Hidden Teacher." *The Unexpected Universe.* New York: Harcourt, 1969.

————. *The Immense Journey.* New York: Vintage, 1959.

Engell, James, and W. Jackson Bate. Editors' Introduction. *Biographia Literaria.* Princeton: Princeton UP, 1983. xli–cxxxvi.

Fish, Stanley. "What Is Stylistics and Why Are They Saying Such Terrible Things about It?" *Is There a Text in This Class?* Cambridge: Harvard UP, 1980. 68–96.

Fishkin, Shelley Fisher. *From Fact to Fiction: Journalism and Imaginative Writing in America.* Baltimore: Johns Hopkins UP, 1985.

Flesch, Rudolf. *The Art of Readable Writing.* 1949. New York: Harper & Row, 1974.

Fletcher, Angus, ed. *The Literature of Fact: Selected Essays from the English Institute.* New York: Columbia UP, 1976.

Flower, Linda S., and John R. Hayes. *A Process Model of Composing.* Pittsburgh: Carnegie-Mellon University, 1979.

Foley, Barbara. *Telling the Truth: The Theory and Practice of Documentary Fiction.* Ithaca: Cornell UP, 1986.

Fort, Keith. "Form, Authority, and the Critical Essay." *College English* 32 (1971): 629–39.

Frye, Northrop. *The Anatomy of Criticism.* Princeton: Princeton UP, 1971.

———. "Myth, Fiction, and Displacement." *Fables of Identity.* New York: Harcourt, 1963. 21–38.

Gardner, Howard. *Art, Mind, and Brain: A Cognitive Approach to Creativity.* New York: Basic Books, 1982.

Goffman, Erving. *Frame Analysis: An Essay on the Organization of Experience.* Cambridge: Harvard UP, 1976.

Gould, Stephen Jay. "Natural Selection and the Human Brain: Darwin *vs.* Wallace." *The Panda's Thumb.* New York: Norton, 1980. 47–58.

Graff, Gerald. "Jargonorama: What We Talk About When We Talk About Lit." *Voice Literary Supplement.* Jan./Feb. 1989: 22, 26.

———. *Poetic Statement and Critical Dogma.* Chicago: U of Chicago P, 1970.

Greenfield, Josh. Rev. of *Armies of the Night,* by Norman Mailer. *Commonweal* 88 (1968): 382.

Grice, H. P. "Logic and Conversation." 1967 Williams James Lectures, Harvard University. Unpub. MS., 1967. Excerpt in *Syntax and Semantics,* Vol. III: *Speech Acts.* Ed. Peter Cole and Jerry L. Morgan. New York: Academic, 1975.

Hellmann, John. *Fables of Fact: The New Journalism as New Fiction.* Urbana: U of Illinois P, 1981.

Herr, Michael. *Dispatches.* New York: Avon, 1978.

Hersey, John. *Hiroshima.* 1946. New York: Bantam, 1948.

Hirsch, E. D., Jr. "What Isn't Literature." *What Is Literature?* Ed. Paul Hernadi. Bloomington: Indiana UP, 1978. 24–34.

Holland, Norman N. *5 Readers Reading.* New Haven: Yale UP, 1975.

Hollowell, John. *Fact and Fiction: The New Journalism and the Nonfiction Novel.* Chapel Hill: U of North Carolina P, 1977.

Horner, Winifred Bryan, ed. *Composition and Literature: Bridging the Gap.* Chicago: U of Chicago P, 1983.

Hough, Graham. *Reflections on a Literary Revolution.* Washington, D.C.: Catholic U of America P, 1960.

Howarth, William L. Introduction. *The John McPhee Reader.* Ed. William L. Howarth. New York: Vintage, 1977. vii–xxxiii.

Iser, Wolfgang. *The Act of Reading: A Theory of Aesthetic Response.* Baltimore: Johns Hopkins UP, 1978.

Jakobson, Roman. "Linguistics and Poetics." *Style in Language.* Ed. Thomas A. Sebeok. Cambridge, MA: MIT, 1960.

James, Henry. "The Art of Fiction." *The Theory of Fiction: Henry James.* Ed. James E. Miller, Jr. Lincoln: U of Nebraska P, 1972. 27–44.

Johnson, Michael L. *The New Journalism: The Underground Press, the Artists of Nonfiction, and Changes in the Established Media.* Lawrence: Kansas UP, 1971.

Kazin, Alfred. Rev. of *Armies of the Night,* by Norman Mailer. *New York Times Book Review* 5 May 1968: 1.

Kinneavy, James L. *A Theory of Discourse.* Englewood Cliffs, NJ: Prentice-Hall, 1971.

Kintsch, Walter. *Psychological Processes in Discourse Production.* Technical Report No. 99. Institute of Cognitive Science. Boulder: U of Colorado, 1980.

———. *The Representation of Meaning in Memory.* Hillsdale, NJ: Erlbaum, 1974.

Kochman, Thomas. *Black and White Styles in Conflict.* Chicago: U of Chicago P, 1981.

Langer, Susanne K. *Philosophy in a New Key.* 1941. New York: New American Library, 1951.

Lanham, Richard. *Literacy and the Survival of Humanism.* New Haven: Yale UP, 1983.

Leavis, F. R. *The Great Tradition.* Garden City, NY: Doubleday, 1954.

Lehman, David, with Ray Sawhill. Rev. of *Bonfire of the Vanities,* by Tom Wolfe. *Newsweek* 26 Oct. 1987: 84–85.

Lemann, Nicholas. Rev. of *Bonfire of the Vanities,* by Tom Wolfe. *The Atlantic* Dec. 1987: 104, 106–7.

Lentricchia, Frank. *After the New Criticism.* Chicago: U of Chicago P, 1980.

Lopez, Barry. *Arctic Dreams: Imagination and Desire in a Northern Landscape.* New York: Scribner's, 1986.

Lyotard, Jean-François. *The Postmodern Condition: A Report on Knowledge.* Trans. Geoff Bennington and Brian Massumi. Minneapolis: U of Minnesota P, 1984.

Mailer, Norman. *Armies of the Night: History as a Novel, the Novel as History.* New York: Signet, 1968.

———. *The Executioner's Song.* Boston: Little, Brown, 1979.

———. Introduction. *In the Belly of the Beast.* By Jack Henry Abbott. New York: Vintage, 1982. ix–xviii.

———. *Marilyn.* New York: Grosset & Dunlap, 1973.

Marius, Richard. *Thomas More.* New York: Vintage, 1985.

Martin, Jay. *Always Merry and Bright: The Life of Henry Miller.* Santa Barbara, CA: Capra Press, 1978.

Matthiessen, Peter. *The Snow Leopard.* New York: Bantam, 1979.

McPhee, John. *Coming Into the Country.* New York: Bantam, 1979.

———. *Rising from the Plains.* New York: Farrar, Straus, Giroux, 1986.

Miller, J. Hillis. *The Ethics of Reading: Kant, de Man, Eliot, Trollope, James, and Benjamin.* New York: Columbia UP, 1987.

Murphy, James E. "The New Journalism: A Critical Perspective." *Journalism Monographs* 34 (1974): 1–30.

Perelman, Chaïm, and L. Olbrechts-Tyteca. *The New Rhetoric: A Treatise on Argumentation.* Trans. John Wilkinson and Purcell Weaver. Notre Dame: Notre Dame UP, 1969.

Podhoretz, Norman. "The Article as Art." *The Reporter as Artist: A Look at the New Journalism Controversy.* Ed. Ronald Weber. New York: Hastings House, 1974.

Pratt, Mary Louise. *Toward a Speech Act Theory of Literary Discourse.* Bloomington: Indiana UP, 1977.

Puzo, Mario. Rev. of *Armies of the Night,* by Norman Mailer. *Book World* 28 Apr. 1968: 1.

Rafferty, Terrence. "The Man Who Knew Too Much." Rev. of *Bonfire of the Vanities,* by Tom Wolfe, *New Yorker* 1 Feb. 1988: 88–92.

Resnik, H. S. Rev. of *Armies of the Night,* by Norman Mailer. *Saturday Review* 4 May 1968: 25.

Richards, I. A. *Practical Criticism.* New York: Harcourt, n.d.

Rosenblatt, Louise. *Literature as Exploration.* 1938. 3rd ed. New York: Noble and Noble, 1976.

——. *The Reader, the Text, the Poem: The Transactional Theory of the Literary Work.* Carbondale: Southern Illinois UP, 1978.

Ross, Lillian. *Picture. Reporting.* New York: Dodd, Mead, 1981. 223–442.

Rousseau, Jean-Jacques. *The Confessions of Jean-Jacques Rousseau.* Anon. trans. of 1783 and 1790 rev. and completed by A. S. B. Glover. New York: Heritage Press, 1955.

Said, Edward. "Opponents, Audiences, Constituencies, and Community." *The Politics of Interpretation.* Ed. W. J. T. Mitchell. Chicago: U of Chicago P, 1983. 7–32.

Saint Augustine. *The Confessions of Saint Augustine.* Trans. J. G. Pilkington. New York: Liveright, 1943.

Scholes, Robert. "Double Perspective on Hysteria." Rev. of *The Electric Kool-Aid Acid Test,* by Tom Wolfe. *Saturday Review* 24 Aug. 1968: 37.

Searle, John. "A Classification of Illocutionary Acts." *Language in Society* 5 (1976): 1–23.

——. *Speech Acts: An Essay in the Philosophy of Language.* Cambridge: Cambridge UP, 1969.

Selzer, Richard. "Diary of an Infidel." *Taking the World in for Repairs.* New York: Morrow, 1986. 13–79.

Smart, Robert Augustin. *The Nonfiction Novel.* Lanham, MD: University Press of America, 1985.

Stone, Irving. *The Passions of the Mind.* New York: Signet, 1972.

Talese, Gay. "Author's Note to Fame and Obscurity." *The Reporter as Artist: A Look at the New Journalism Controversy.* Ed. Ronald Weber. New York: Hastings House, 1974. 35–38.

——. *Honor Thy Father.* New York: Dell, 1981.

——. *The Kingdom and the Power.* New York: Dell, 1981.

Tannen, Deborah. "Oral and Literate Strategies in Spoken and Written Discourse." *Literacy for Life: The Demand for Reading and Writing.* Ed. Richard W. Bailey and Robin Melanie Fosheim. New York: The Modern Language Association of America, 1983. 79–96.

Tate, Allen. "Literature as Knowledge." *Critical Theory Since Plato.* Ed. Hazard Adams. New York: Harcourt, 1971. 927–41.

Taylor, M. Martin, and Insup Taylor. *The Psychology of Reading.* San Diego: Academic, 1983.

Thomas, Lewis. *Late Night Thoughts on Listening to Mahler's Ninth Symphony.* New York: Bantam, 1984.

Thompson, Hunter S. *The Curse of Lono.* New York: Bantam, 1983.

———. *Fear and Loathing in Las Vegas: A Savage Journey to the Heart of the American Dream.* New York: Warner, 1971.

———. *Fear and Loathing on the Campaign Trail.* San Francisco: Straight Arrow Books, 1973.

———. *The Great Shark Hunt.* New York: Warner, 1982.

———. *Hell's Angels.* New York: Ballantine, 1967.

Thompson, Thomas. *Blood and Money.* New York: Dell, 1976.

Tompkins, Jane P., ed. *Reader-Response Criticism: From Formalism to Post-Structuralism.* Baltimore: Johns Hopkins UP, 1980.

Toulmin, Stephen. *The Uses of Argument.* Cambridge, Eng.: Cambridge UP, 1958.

Tulving, Endel. "Episodic and Semantic Memory." *Organization of Memory.* Ed. Endel Tulving and Wayne Donaldson. New York: Academic, 1972.

van Dijk, Teun A. *Macrostructures: An Interdisciplinary Study of Global Structure in Discourse, Interaction, and Cognition.* Hillsdale, NJ: Erlbaum, 1980.

Wambaugh, Joseph. *The Onion Field.* New York: Dell, 1973.

Weber, Ronald. *The Literature of Fact.* Athens: Ohio UP, 1980.

Wellek, René. "What Is Literature?" *What Is Literature.* Ed. Paul Hernadi. Bloomington: Indiana UP, 1978. 16–23.

Wellek, René, and Austin Warren. *Theory of Literature.* New York: Harcourt, 1956.

Wheelwright, Philip. "The Logical and the Translogical." *Critical Theory Since Plato.* Ed. Hazard Adams. New York: Harcourt, 1971. 1102–12.

White, Hayden. "The Fictions of Factual Representation." *The Literature of Fact: Selected Essays from the English Institute.* Ed. Angus Fletcher. New York: Columbia UP, 1976.

Williams, Raymond. *Marxism and Literature.* Oxford and New York: Oxford UP, 1977.

Winterowd, W. Ross. "Brain, Rhetoric, and Style." *Linguistics, Stylistics, and the Teaching of Composition.* Ed. Donald McQuade. Akron: U of Akron P, 1979.

———. *Composition/Rhetoric: A Synthesis.* Carbondale: Southern Illinois UP, 1986.

Witte, Stephen P., and Lester Faigley. "Coherence, Cohesion, and Writing Quality." *College Composition and Communication* 32 (1981): 189–204.

Wolfe, Tom. *Bonfire of the Vanities.* New York: Farrar, Straus, Giroux, 1987.

———. *The Kandy-Kolored Tangerine-Flake Streamline Baby.* New York: Pocket Books, 1966.

———. "Las Vegas (What?) Las Vegas (Can't Hear You! Too Noisy!) Las Vegas!!!!" *The Kandy-Kolored Tangerine-Flake Streamline Baby.* New York: Pocket Books, 1966. 3–24.

———. "The New Journalism." *The New Journalism.* Ed. Tom Wolfe and E. W. Johnson. New York: Harper & Row, 1973.

———. *The Right Stuff.* New York: Farrar, Straus, Giroux, 1979.

Zavarzadeh, Mas'ud. *The Mythopoeic Reality: The Postwar American Nonfiction Novel.* Urbana: U of Illinois P, 1976.

Zeiger, William. "The Exploratory Essay: Enfranchising the Spirit of Inquiry in College Composition." *College English* 47 (1985): 454–66.

Index

W. Ross Winterowd is Bruce R. McElderry Professor of English at the University of Southern California, where he founded the graduate program in rhetoric, linguistics, and literature. The author of *Composition/Rhetoric: A Synthesis* and *The Culture and Politics of Literacy*, he is currently researching the epistemological, disciplinary, and political background of reading and writing in the American academic establishment.